T0198494

Other books by Fred R. Lybrand

*Heavenly Citizenship: The Spiritual
Alternative to Power Politics*

*The Absolute Quickest Way to Help
Your Child Change*

About Life and Uganda

Insights From A Short-term Pilgrim

 www.trafford.com

North America & international
toll-free: 1 888 232 4444 (USA & Canada)
fax: 812 355 4082

To *Joanna Holmes White Lybrand,*
better known as Jody to us all... a Southern Belle
with the charm and grace to endure me as I've grown
up over time...I love you and dedicate this work to you,
my sweet, as we labor in our Lord's work together.
Your gift helped me focus on penning these words,
because so many details in our life are cared for by your
uncomplaining help.

ACKNOWLEDGEMENTS

There are so many people to thank for their contribution to this small work; however, I want to limit my thanks to just three special groups-

- **Mbale Presbyterian Church** in Eastern Uganda with Morris and Aidah Ogenga. These are the faithful souls who began to dream and continue to keep the vision alive for us all.

- **Grace Community Bible Church** in Northern Fort Ben County (Houston) with my dear friend, Dr. Keith Bower. This is the church which first shared the vision with us, allowed us to tag along, and continues to broadcast the dream to all who will listen.

- **Midland Bible Church** in Midland, Texas. This is the place my family and I have found as a true home, filled with friends and co-laborers in Christ, who together, saw the vision happen.

Thank you for your love, your example, and your ability to look ahead...you each have given the gift of a new choice to a multitude.

EXORDIUM

As cold water to a weary soul,
So is good news from a far country.   *(Proverbs 25:25)*

I like to keep in mind what Sydney Smith observed, **"The writer does the most who gives his reader the most knowledge and takes from him the least time."** I hope you'll find what I've sought to pen here is that very thing; a book where, though you may read it once quickly, the insights will invite you to read it again and again. It is in this sense that you are about to read a book about LIFE. Knowledge, insight, lessons, principles; it all comes to the same important point. In John 8, Jesus observed that freedom springs from the deep waters of the knowledge of the truth. I hope these thoughts, and the included good news from a far country, is a cool drink to your soul.

This book is also about a foreign land called Uganda. The lessons here could have been picked up anywhere; however, they were not from anywhere. These insights are from a special place where grace is alive.

ix

If you picked up this book because it sounded interesting, you're probably not the first person I hoped would read it. You may, however, be the one who can recommend it to that person, and benefit on the way.

The person I have in mind is fed up, or at least pretty irritated, when he hears about missions overseas. This type tends to either disappear without a noise when "foreign missions" arises as a topic or, God-forbid, a missionary speaks at church. He can also be heard saying such things as, "There are plenty of people right here in America to reach, why don't we reach them?" - or, "We could use that money to help people here instead of sending it so far away... it doesn't seem to be a good stewardship of money."

The trouble is, I basically agree with these people. They have a point. I used to be one of them and had my point too. Now, however, God has graced me to see some things I couldn't see before. I consider it a breath of new life for me personally, and for our church's vibrancy as a body of believers in Jesus Christ.

We are moving from being flat toward pointedly offering the gospel. We are moving from "ho-hum" Christianity to "how can" faith in Christ. We are less often asking questions like, "Why aren't people excited about missions and sharing their faith?" Now we are asking questions like, "How can we do more than we're doing?"

We don't claim to have the answers for you, your church, or your life, but we do have our expanding experience to share with you. This little volume is in your hands to offer the single most important solution we've found to turning our church and our lives toward kindly sharing the message of God's love and grace. It all comes to a single word: *INVOLVEMENT.*

The moment you become involved in fulfilling the Great Commission can be a moment of genuine transformation. It isn't the preaching or the plan, but the actual hands-on involvement of the people that begins the change. Drop the "Why?" question and pick up the "How?"

How can we begin to INVOLVE more people in Missions?

When you begin to ask this question with your church leaders and faithful church members, you will see the possibilities appear before your eyes and for your heart. The following thoughts are a small window through which to see how God has begun to move us to consider those outside of Christ.

These notes *About Life and Uganda* are my reflections and observations offered to encourage your walk with Christ, your pursuit of wisdom, and your church's expanded contribution of grace in this world.

God Bless,

Fred R. Lybrand
Midland, Texas

CONTENTS

Part I: *About Uganda*

Part II: *About Life*

ABOUT UGANDA

I

THE GIFT

"Why is this dirty-from-working Ugandan woman giving me an egg?" I wondered as her wrinkled hands offered up to me the lightly cupped present. "It's a gift," my translator said, "for coming and sharing from God's Word with her."

I looked at her with amazement and then confusion. In part I was exaggerating and in part I was trying to communicate. I was about to say something honest...and shocking.

Only moments before I had carefully walked her through the gospel of God's grace, the very reason I came to Uganda. The day is humid, I am standing in an opening with two huts, and the wind is only moving the highest leaves of the nearest banana tree, with green everywhere in my sight except on the gray thatched roof and the dark dirt path we followed to this place. We sit on a grass mat, no chair means greater poverty, I assume, and I notice how much this place feels like the green I knew as a boy in Alabama, but I could be anywhere. Where I am does not matter, just this dear woman, her kids scurry about in the background, trying to listen and remain unheard, attending to the babies, in-tow on a back and happy enough just to be carried about.

She looks down as she answers my questions, looking down being a way to show respect and I remember David in his song in Psalm 131,

> "LORD, my heart is not haughty,
> Nor my eyes lofty.
> Neither do I concern myself with great matters,
> Nor with things too profound for me.

She is not haughty as she shows me great deference. Most of the women in Uganda seem to do this very thing. She is very genuine and sweet in her countenance and her quiet answers to my questions about her own spiritual journey. Her eyes keep looking down as she plays with a stick on the mat, drawing short circles and tall circles swished back and forth, but more like miniature performers on ice, not exactly stopping, but re-gathering speed to move from one end of the show floor to another. She has surely never seen ice on a lake or a floor, or the beauty of two bodies united in a graceful dance. But she sees something as her eyes follow her twig.

I explain the truth of Christ and the life-eternal He offers to all who believe in Him. She is listening and responding and I think she will be like the men we just left in a plowed field, two men whose enthusiasm was almost more than I could stand. "Please come to my house and share this with my children. They will be out of school soon," he tells me through the translator. His eyes, teeth, and heart are all bright. Years ago some missionaries came to his village and began a church... and oh so happy were they all until the day the missionaries left and the meetings died and the tree as the place to meet for lessons and services became just another tree on the way to or on the way from.

I share with him that we will leave a building as a true church home (he knows about it) and a Pastor from among his own people who will not leave, but will remain and teach the Word of God to any and all who want to learn. He is grateful and uncontained.

This woman before me just now on the mat with the ice capade at the end of her switch is about to express the same joy, the same thrill, the same exuberance...but she says, "Not yet." Not yet? "Do you believe that Christ was crucified, died, buried and was raised for you?" Not yet. "Do you believe that He will give everlasting life to those who believe in Him?" Not yet.

She does not believe, not yet, but she hurries into her hut to bring me an egg to thank me for the most important message I know to share with another human being, a message that she gives me an egg to have heard, and a "not yet" also to take with me.

It is here that I shock her with my question. A very sincere question, directed at a woman who I think of as simply another human being in need of a resurrected Savior. I ask her a question just as if it had been any neighbor in the United States.

"May I ask a question?" I say and she responds through the translator "Yes", with the egg still held high for my eyes. "I offered you a gift of eternal life through Christ, to which you said, 'No'. Why do you now offer me a gift and expect me to say, 'Yes'?" She listens as he translates, and she looks a bit confused as I reissue the question, "Why should I accept this gift you offer me when you reject the gift I offer you?"

She and I are both struck by the question. I take the egg and invite her to remember that the salvation offered in Christ is a gift for her to receive just as I received her egg.

I walk away from her hut sad but noticing more green and less gray, or brown, or dirt-dark trail. It feels more like Alabama than ever because people seemed more like people than ever. A see-through feeling swells in my heart as I realize something a bit further about this effort in Uganda. This woman had declined. She had not believed, at least, not yet. Was she within her rights? Yes. Must she believe? Not for me. And this is the great point I saw...in the midst of so many people coming to Christ...those who say "no" show what we are seeing with the gospel is not a cultural politeness. It is not simply that everyone in Uganda nicely says "yes"—rather it is a work on the human heart, perhaps en masse, but not for all. No matter how things sometime seem, faith in Christ remains a broadly personal decision.

Then He said to Thomas, "Reach your finger here, and look at My hands; and reach your hand here, and put it into My side. Do not be unbelieving, but believing." And Thomas answered and said to Him, "My Lord and my God!" Jesus said to him, "Thomas, because you have seen Me, you have believed. Blessed are those who have not seen and yet have believed." (John 20:27-29)

II

THE BEGINNING

"It seems easier just to start over," I said. We'd been wrestling for some time over an ongoing problem for our church. What do you do about Missions? We had noticed a trend for many years, and with the obvious needs of so many on a day-in-day-out basis, it was easy, even simple, to ignore the problem. The problem itself was that whenever one of our missionaries came to speak during a service or special event, people would scatter. Listening to a missionary to our average member was like playing Big Band swing music to the average American teen. Just the thought was enough to cause the ashen response of an anxiety attack. Why would missions, a well-known and important work for any "Bible-believing" church, keep people away? As a pastor/elder at Midland Bible Church in Midland, Texas, I'm guessing I'm not alone on this concern.

In thinking about this whole issue, fortunately, it never crossed our minds to blame the members of the

Church. Leadership often seeks to blame the members (just as the members try to blame the leaders), but a basic principle we've tried to follow is that the Church goes where the leaders take it. I had an even more personal reason not to blame the members. *I felt the same way.* Many missionaries made me want to scream! "Ooh," they'd say. "The work is so wonderful. See my pictures. God has really blessed us." And they'd drone on with tiresome stories of lands far away and tales that weren't intriguing or particularly impressive either. It seemed so far away from my life and the burdens and challenges I face daily. The challenges I face as a "minister of the gospel" in America seemed ignored by most of my encounters with missionaries. They seemed to just skip over the difficulties we face in our own nation, and in our own churches; causing such a disconnection that it felt like watching a Sci-Fi flick about an other-than-here world. Of course, chances are they felt the exact same way.

On top all of this, most missionaries I'd met left me feeling that laboring for Christ in America was less noble than laboring abroad; not to mention their freedom to criticize the American Church for being too fat, lukewarm, self-centered, lazy, psychological, etc. It is so easy to misjudge and hold things in a place of suspicion and critique. And yet, even as I write, I'm criticizing those who also seek to serve the Lord. I'm embarrassed for both those who have said such things and for myself, as we will all stand, or at least appear, before the Judgment Seat of Christ. Romans 14:10-13 comes to mind as a sound and appropriate rebuke;

But why do you judge your brother? Or why do you show contempt for your brother? For we shall all stand before the judgment seat of Christ. For it is written:

> *"As I live, says the LORD,*
> *Every knee shall bow to Me,*
> *And every tongue shall confess to God."*

So then each of us shall give account of himself to God. Therefore let us not judge one another anymore, but rather resolve this, not to put a stumbling block or a cause to fall in our brother's way.

Our story continues.

"I think we should fire them." I remember that moment when I came to the conclusion and announced it rather matter-of-factly to the other Elders. I serve with a team of spiritually qualified individuals...no decision is made without full agreement...no agreement means we pray more.

"Fire them?" someone said. "Well," I replied, "I'm overstating it for effect, but until we let go of our current missionaries, we will never think straight about missions."

Let's gain a little history here. Midland Bible Church, for starters, is a bit of a strange duck, as churches go. For example, I teach from the Bible for about 45 minutes every Sunday. We added our first true "staff" member after thirteen years, wanting to first get the ministry of the Church firmly in the hands and hearts of the members before we added "hired guns" to

8

do the work. Now, as we add staff, they will serve to support the ministries in place, along with equipping others for new ministries. Historically, we are most closely related to the Baptists and Presbyterians...but Christian is our preferred term for ourselves. We are not particularly interested in changing the world politically, but we do labor to change individuals personally and spiritually. Change may not be the right word, but our hope is to create a context in which individuals, marriages, and families all grow well in this less-than-perfect world. Finally, our ongoing theme is "grace and truth", which we find bothers a lot of people in one way or another. We avoid legalism and external constraints to get people to take action, rather emphasizing the transformation of the human heart toward a life that honors God. This really bothers some who place "obedience" in the supreme position. We also, however, don't tend to compromise on the truth, another often-distasteful thing for many who have pre-decided what God, life, and church is all about. In my 16 years in Midland, we have added about a million and a half dollars worth of buildings, and have never passed a plate in a service. Not even once. I'm not proposing that this is how churches should be; rather I'm telling you how we are.

Nonetheless, God has assembled a pretty wonderful group of individuals who have made this church and this community their true home. We've seen many people change jobs, or even careers, in order to stay here. It is certainly one of the most gratifying things in my own life to have stayed through trials to see

God's good work first hand in one place. Uganda, however, has let us personally see God's good work in another place as well.

Yes, we "fired our missionaries". Though all of our missionaries are good people, things needed to change. Our frustration with missions goes back many years. Like most churches, we inherited our missionaries from our forefathers and added a few of our own. They were missionaries scattered from America to Mexico to Europe to the Far East. Occasionally they would drop through and share with the church about their labors abroad. Usually this meant the church would see a surprising drop in attendance for that Sunday. Additionally, some of our missionaries would "inform us" about career decisions and moves they were making to a different place or different purpose altogether.

Needless to say, this didn't sit well with us, because in the course of time we had developed a growing conviction that we wanted to be a part of certain results abroad, not just a financing institution for a collection of individuals. Furthermore, we were concerned about the overall lack of burden for missions among our members. This lack of burden, we concluded, came from a lack of interest in sharing the good news with others who were interested and open to it.

We gave our missionaries one year's severance pay and asked God to show us how to match missions with our church.

What happened next surprised even us...we went
to Uganda.[1]

---

[1]For a summary of our process in Uganda, see Appendices 4
and 5 on pp. 127-129.

III

UNDECORATED SIMPLICITY

He walks with the gait of a 13 year-old boy, not a man as such, but not a boy either, almost swinging, backpack in tow; cap on...up and frayed the cool way now...the limp from his long-had cerebral palsy can't be noticed in the uneven terrain. Through patches of sweet potatoes, around the brackish mud holes where the trail submerges, we trod along through a neighbor's field until we arrive.

She hurries to bring small wooden chairs, homemade and handmade, but sturdy, giving me the largest chair and my son Tripp, the 13 year-old, a smaller but perfect-for-him seat.

Moses and Ceadric, our guides and translators had agreed to give this son of mine his opportunity; and he takes it, not hesitating but starting right in to share the gospel with this man and two women in the heart of a land and people we only knew through the news and the guesses our imagination leaped to make.

Africa, Uganda specifically, is not like I imagined, not thinking but listening as Tripp opens the conversation with these gentle and hardworking people in the village of Namaje, our church-planting location. "Has anyone ever taken a Bible and shown you how to know for sure you're going to heaven?" The man looks intently at Moses who translates with gestures and smiles, calmly not like a car salesmen but intently as a Pastor, which he is when not helping with the work in another part of his country.

The man makes no noticeable sound or motion, but Moses looks to Tripp and declares no one has. My son politely asks, "May I?" And Moses translates and the man says "yes" without saying or doing anything. Such is the way with the villagers in Uganda, no disagreement meaning agreement, interspersed with "hmmm" going from a soft low sound to an even lower sound...yes he understands or yes he agrees...but in this instance no sound means, "Please tell me this message...you who have brought me the Word of God from such a faraway place...you who are the reason I have stopped my work to listen."

Tripp explains the message further sharing that there is both Good News and Bad News...the Good News is something about God, the Bad News, something about us.

As Tripp shares the message of God's grace, I first think how methodical and "textbook" he is about the whole matter, moving from point to point just as he was taught and just as he believes is appropriate. It's almost too formal, I think as Moses translates just as

13

Tripp speaks, and yet I quickly shift from evaluating how well my son is doing to begin praying for the hearts of those listening people in front of us. A father, perhaps 40 years old, faded blue shorts, dirty with dirty legs and hands, somewhat apologetic, but he has been working in the garden, as they call it, the substance of their existence...Uganda is a temperate and tropical place and if rain comes all is well, for the ground will grow almost anything. Banana trees are nearby, along with potatoes or corn (maize as they say), and a variety of trees like mango and jackfruit. Somewhere beyond us they grow sugar cane; I see it strapped to bicycles on the way to home or market and tried it later myself...sweet wood which is chewy but flavorful...and I look at this dirty man and see no dirt, but a man like me yet one who is willing to listen to a 13 year-old boy tell him the news that could soon usher him into eternity.

Nearby is his wife and many steps away his daughter-in-law who is not allowed to sit close to her husband's father...I think it is at first silly but then wise as a tradition because these people are just like us...people who struggle against the danger we see in forms at the office and the gym because families are so little together in America... and I know we are not the moral compass for anyone though once I might have been tempted to believe in us.

Today I believe in Christ and the message my son continues to share. It is a message of GIFT that reaches beyond the moral and the immoral to the heart of God, the giver of all good things, who gave His Son and gave me my son to share in telling a man my age of this gift of life through Christ.

I don't have time to be amazed, that will come later as now I pray because Tripp has come to a crucial point in the message...having gone past the reality that we are all spiritually dead in our sin, past the truth that our sin confirms our desserts apart from God in the future, and past the hope offered by the Son's death in our place.

"For God so loved the world that He gave..." echoes in my mind as I notice that all eyes are downward, studying their own hearts as a downward look allows us not to look but to see beyond the ground and through the other side of the earth, past the stars and universe, past this dimension to our own lives, our hearts which are certainly and definitely within but seem, by implication, to have consequences so "out there" as to demand a glance, even a gaze, beyond us to the universal hope all but the most cynical have in a life beyond this one. A better life. A better existence. A place of both finality and beginnings we know is the perfection we have sought but have never found in this life and on this earth. As Augustine said in some form, "Our hearts find no rest until they rest in Thee."

I see three human beings at the edge of finding perfection, not by achievement or their own hapless efforts, but from receiving the gift of perfection into their own lives through the person of Jesus Christ.

The gift of perfection was made available to us through death. A strange notion and difficult to explain: this thing death. Everyone knows in sober moments his own mortality, but in a land where death is a constant fact, not hidden away from plain sight in the funeral home parlors of our land, these people see death up close and personal...who escapes seeing a baby or two, a spouse, a friend succumb to malaria or cholera or AIDS or a simple infection that consumes a body from an untreated wound? No one escapes, at least, not in Uganda. Death is a constant and continual illustration to make the dying of a Man in their place a quick fact to grasp. "What does it mean for Christ to die for you?" These people hope they know but listen intently to Tripp explain. "Suppose you had a terrible disease in your body." I hear Moses translate with unknown syllables until he gets to the word for disease where he distinctly uses the word AIDS.

Tripp continues, "But what if I knew a great doctor who could take the disease out of you and put it into me? You would live but I would die." I think Tripp should be more passionate or use better inflection, but he says to them in a matter-of-fact way that makes sense...it makes sense because it has the very thing he has heard since the day of his birth. It makes sense because he believes it and because he has embraced it for himself...and I think of Romans 1:16 which says the gospel itself is the power of God. No inflection, no illustration, no greatness in the presenter gives the power to deliver people from death to life; it is in the gospel alone. I silence my mind and remember to pray. "It represents what Christ did for us as it says in Romans 5:8, 'But God demonstrates His own love toward us, in that while we were still sinners, Christ died for us.'"

Tripp has hardly spoken and already he is to his point. What a gentle rebuke for the Lord to me and so many of us who try to make the gospel into a symphony, when in fact, it is a melody.

Now Tripp crisply offers, as he has crisply offered all along, the crescendo of the whole of the gospel. "Ephesians 2:8&9 says, 'For by grace you have been saved through faith, and that not of yourselves it is the gift of God; not of works lest anyone should boast.' All you have to do is believe. Before I sat in this chair I didn't look at it and inspect it...I had faith, I believed that it would hold me up. So, if we believe that Christ's death paid the penalty for our sins, then we can be sure of eternal life."

It is funny, maybe strange or sad, that so much stir has been made over time about works and faith and fruit, but I know that it is all part of a cosmic battle for the souls of men and women alike...what a silly notion that mere faith in the act of a dead-but-we-believe-resurrected man would secure our destiny forever in God. And yet, it does. It is this cornerstone of simple faith that is the great stumbling block for mankind. We all know that what we do determines what we get, but in God's great reversal He offers the only thing that make sense to children and the simpleminded...and does not make sense to the wise thinker of this age or any age...since now our works are seen by God as filthy rags, what else but simple faith would strip all glory away from us and posit it appropriately on the God of creation? It is not a special kind of faith that saves, but a simple faith in a very special Person.

Tripp asks next, "Is there anything stopping you from believing this?" There is only a short pause and the man in the blue shorts speaks a soft single syllable word, Moses saying something to each of the two women who even softer speak a syllable. "There is nothing," Moses says as he looks to Tripp to lead.

My son, leading at thirteen, is an amazing and wonderful thought as we watch these three newfound siblings in Christ follow my son in a prayer to express their gratitude for God's gift of His Son. Tripp makes it clear that it is not a prayer but faith, alone, that saves them and they smile as they are ready to follow. . . *"Jesus, I admit I'm a sinner in need of a Savior. Thank you that you died on a cross for me, and were raised from the dead. I believe in you and, by faith, I thank you for the gift of salvation and forgiveness...and for making me truly a child of God."* Now as I type these words I know that words on paper are incapable of showing anyone the beauty of that moment as boy and men and women knelt together in the plush and simple homeland of a heart-hungry people...for one glorious instant, joined together in Christ with nothing mattering on the entire planet or in our lifetime history, except this one clear event of God adding to His fold the lost sheep who were found and reclaimed by the One who loved them from before Genesis 1:1.

Above all, this may explain why people who encounter the love of God through Jesus Christ are never the same...and as they follow Him, are touched by moments like my moment in a small village in Uganda...never to be the same, all over again.

IV

MY PERSONAL NOTES

What can you learn from personally going to the mission field? There are nine primary things I learned from my firsthand experience. I have recorded them just as they were written in my notebook. I've left them in this form because it seems to catch a little more of the honest sloppiness most of us have when we record our thoughts. As we view them one by one, I'll put them in a more proper form. I don't know what you will learn, but these lessons were what God had for me.

July 24, 2001 (as originally written)

After a long and grueling trip, I'm writing after a thorough night's sleep. We are home and all is well with the church, the children, and us. I am well too and want to record my observations / reflections.

1. God will answer my prayers as specifically as I ask them & just as I ask them (answer = "yes!"). I need only (i) follow the Spirit; and (ii) ask according to my heart.

2. I have asked & I am receiving greater and greater measures of earnestness for my preaching.

3. All people are the same...exactly the same. Culture only puts a spin on the "sameness".

4. Limits Yield Intensity: Our focused time helped us focus as Christians. We prayed for each speaker, in person, in a circle around him / her.

5. Christianity may be (& is to be) lived at all times.

6. Rather than comparing and criticizing the believers at home (vs. Uganda) ~ I believe we should encourage Christians to move up to the next level! The aim: To live is Christ!

7. The Word of God can always be fresh to me ~ I need only open it & read...& open my heart and listen.

8. I remain embarrassed ~ to whom much is given, much is expected. I am choosing to increase my faithfulness to my Lord by closing the distance between what God has gifted me with & how I am using it (Full Amount direct toward the Right

Things before God). Additionally, increasing my faithfulness includes cultivating & following my heart in Christ.

9. *The single most important / impactful thing I can do is to preach the Word (Earnestly as an oracle of God...1 Peter 4:10-11).*

What do you make of these? Well, for me they are rather personal, and may be the things you learned in spiritual First Grade. First Grade or not, they are all one of the two basic experiences we have as we encounter Truth.

I have discovered it is very important to understand that there are two responses we can have to truth. Of course, there's a third one if you include Churchill's observation that, "Most people stumble over the truth and get up and move on as if nothing happened." The two options are what I call "Ah-ha" and "Oh-yeah".

Ah-ha

Ah-ha(s) are great. We long for them and look for them and feel as though we are the first person God ever showed the particular truth at hand. It is a great discovery and we know it is a treasure, a treasure to be shared with others; and if we're young or brave we tell someone at a study or by phone or in a letter...but share it we must. Ah-has are those truths that hit us at a point of need, and just like water to a wilted houseplant we come back to life for a moment. A famous example of this encounter with truth is found in Luke 24:25-32 on the road to Emmaus,

> Then He said to them, "O foolish ones, and slow of heart to believe in all that the prophets have spoken! Ought not the Christ to have suffered these things and to enter into His glory?" And beginning at Moses and all the Prophets, He expounded to them in all the Scriptures the things concerning Himself.
>
> Then they drew near to the village where they were going, and He indicated that He would have gone farther. But they constrained Him, saying, "Abide with us, for it is toward evening, and the day is far spent." And He went in to stay with them.
>
> Now it came to pass, as He sat at the table with them, that He took bread, blessed and broke it, and gave it to them. Then their eyes were opened and they knew Him; and He vanished from their sight.
>
> And they said to one another, "Did not our heart burn within us while He talked with us on the road, and while He opened the Scriptures to us?"

In this instance the two were hit with a double Ah-ha. The first mentioned is the greater; they had been in the presence of Jesus Christ, resurrected. The second is how the truth of God's Word burned in their hearts as He opened the Scriptures to them.

Throughout the Bible we see individuals, and sometimes groups, waking up to a particular truth or insight. Sometimes an Ah-ha is more of a negative response to a newly seen truth. We might call these "Oh-no(s)", and we see an example when Christ explains the seriousness of the marriage covenant from God's viewpoint; and the disciples respond by saying in Matthew 19:10,

> His disciples said to Him, "If such is the case of the man with his wife, it is better not to marry."

"Oh-no" they say. "All cannot accept this saying," is Christ's simple response. Responding to truth when it jars you is only one response. There is a second response.

Oh-Yeah

"Oh-Yeah(s)" are neither as dramatic nor as exhilarating as the joy of discovery in an Ah-ha. Oh-Yeahs, however, may be even more vital for our understanding and growth in the Lord. An Oh-Yeah is a renewed awareness of something already known. It is the recovery of an old truth that you had not, until the point of rediscovery, noticed it applied to your current situation. Two famous Oh-Yeahs verses come from the words of Paul and Peter.

> **Paul:** *Finally, my brethren, rejoice in the Lord. For me to write the same things to you is not tedious, but for you it is safe. Beware of dogs, beware of evil workers... (Philippians 3:1-2)*

Peter: *Yes, I think it is right, as long as I am in this tent, to stir you up by reminding you..., (2 Peter 1:13) Beloved, I now write to you this second epistle (in both of which I stir up your pure minds by way of reminder), that you may be mindful of the words which were spoken before by the holy prophets, and of the commandment of us, the apostles of the Lord and Savior, knowing this first: that scoffers will come in the last days... (2 Peter 3:1)*

Both apostles are well aware that they have spoken these truths before or that the readers know these truths already. They are not deterred, however, because the importance of the truth calls for a reminder. Oftentimes we do not bring to the forefront of our awareness the truth or understanding we need. At this point, God will often bring a needed reminder to us, directly or indirectly, that we may again grasp it for a fresh application.

We can imagine the readers of these letters from Paul and Peter, with some look of embarrassment toward one another, exclaim, "Duh". Well perhaps not "duh", but something on the order of "Oh-Yeah". We are quick to forget, and indeed in these examples, we are quick to forget what misguidance is often just at the next bend, or the next door, or in the next person.

My experience in Uganda was not of this sort. It was not a trip to remind me of danger, but to remind me of neglect. Jesus, Himself, observed that "to whom much is given, much is expected" (one of my Oh-Yeahs). My short-term experience was to remind me of nine simple truths that work because they are true, and because they are right; because they belong to the will and way of God, and the universe He created.

These nine truths included both surprising Ah-has and valuable Oh-Yeahs for me. Perhaps they will catch you by surprise as well. The first lesson may be the only one you need. The first lesson is ...

ABOUT LIFE

V

GOD TENDS TO ANSWER PRAYER AS SPECIFICALLY AS YOU ASK

It was the same day I saw a man mow the grass with a machete. I spent the morning there, on the landscaped estate of the Mt. Elgon Hotel. The grass is a green sea washing up to the circling white wall forming a safe boundary beyond which I see huts; and beyond huts I see roads, and then, the rising mountains toward Elgon, and beyond that, Kenya. I write about what I see, and the man with the machete, and the Ugandan coffee is perfect—so I bathe in my decision not to go with the group. They are off to see waterfalls and other sites because it is Saturday and the work is done except for tonight's crusade and the opening Sunday service where I will preach on the importance of community to the individual's spirit. I think it is something the Ugandan villagers will understand quickly, not like Americans, who are so restaurant crazed that they shop for churches and spouses like they do the best new place to eat. I wonder how we convinced ourselves that church is a show and not a family, but I remember what we have in Midland—not perfect—not perfect at all, but a surprising group who have changed careers and perspectives to belong together as a family of God, both suffering and rejoicing, just as God invites us. It is a church in the most perfect, yet most youthful form my study and imagination can see.

I think about Jody and Tripp, mother and son both born on the 15th of November, forever sharing that beginning date and this beginning trip to offer grace to the people in this rebuilding part of central Africa. I think of them because I have finished my sermon preparation, I have prayed for Sunday, I have written the thoughts I had been holding all week for Saturday. It is past one o'clock, past two o'clock, past three o'clock and they have not returned. The time they were due was lunch—in town—dropping by our hotel to freshen up and to retrieve me.

I try not to worry, but I am in a foreign country and my wife and son and many friends are out and hours late. My vivid mind's eye can see the accident and the deadly result and the solemn trip home and the words to the other children, four in all, with no mother, no brother, and service-for-God to blame. I catch myself and steady up remembering that "Uganda Time" is not like America. Late is never late and early is as absent as snow in this tropical land. But I still feel worry creep on top of me and I say aloud, "Fred, you don't know what has happened—worry when you know something definite."

I've been trained well and have counseled hundreds that we "know what we know and don't know what we don't know". Anything could have happened, or nothing at all. Besides, in all things, God's providence is unthwarted. I wait again for another hour and my worry comes to a fevered pitch. Since I emphasize prayer I stoop to pray. The time for the crusade is near and lunch is hours past. I prayed these exact words,

"Lord, please perform a miracle and have the vans pull up as I walk out the front door of the hotel."

I really prayed nothing else except my attitude was apologetic for my lack of trust and my desperate need to know all is well, and that my wife and my son are happily intact.

I walk downstairs and steadily move to the entrance while I only distantly hear some conversation within the halls and ignore a quiet attendant at the front desk. I only look at my foot—steady ahead, reaching for the first step. Indeed, my only goal following my prayer is to touch the first step and I do, and I look to the parking lot. One van has stopped, the other pulls in next to it and I see all smiles, tired smiles. Everyone is safe and Uganda time prevails as I quietly thank God with the slight odor of unbelief around me—God so faithful, by providence, by request, by coincidence—but my prayer was answered exactly; and I think, "What a patient and strategic God we serve to underscore a simple truth by drawing me across the world for a week of wonder to see this lesson repeated in weather, results, safety, and countless small moments of specific answers."

God Tends To Answer Prayer As Specifically As You Ask

Why do we see so little answered prayer? People have their theories and write volumes for us to glean a reason for our failing prayer life. Usually the complaint against us is a lack of faith. Who can argue with something so unfalsifiable (by unfalsifiable I mean—you can't prove it false, so you can't prove it true). I, you, we, do not have enough faith; and who can argue since Christianity is a faith into which we are born, walk, and die graciously by faith. We never have enough faith, but all we need is a speck, a mustard seed. Is your prayer unanswered? You didn't believe enough, so they say...and who can argue?

Others instruct us that God always answers. He says "yes". He says "no". He says "not yet". And again we find that people explain our lack of answered prayer as a simple misperception— it's a diamond we've mistaken for a dirty rock. With this kind of correction to give us fresh and disbelieving eyes we say, "Ah, the Lord's will be done...thanks for Thy answer we receive from Thy bountiful hand"—even though God said, "No!"

Honestly, what do we mean by "answered prayer"? When I speak of God answering my prayers I mean He answered, "Yes!" I only mean this and you only mean this too. It is time, high time as they say from our part of the world, that we quit twisting prayer away from what it is and what we mean.

"God, it's me, please do this thing this way. Amen."

Now that is a prayer form. It is no formula, but it is a shape that gets to the point. We want God to answer our prayers by saying "yes" and doing it! Now is that so hard to admit? I know it is for some who have taken God's attributes through a sieve and fished out all but His omnipotence and sovereignty. But look at what John tells us in his gospel,

> *"And in that day you will ask Me nothing. Most assuredly, I say to you, whatever you ask the Father in My name He will give you. Until now you have asked nothing in My name. Ask, and you will receive, that your joy may be full." (John 16:23-24)*

Not only are we (by extension) promised to receive exactly what we ask for; we are told that the aim of answered prayer is **our own joy**. Our joy? Absolutely. It may shake up your theology, philosophy, worldview, and recipe for lasagna—but God actually has as the aim of your praying—your very joy! It's quite simple. God, the Father, derives delight (merely from our praying—Proverbs 15:8) and joy when He gives to His own the exact things that will bring them joy. Indeed, I often tell the Father exactly what joy the answer will mean to me. I make it a stated part of my prayers that I will rejoice when He says, "Yes," and gives me the very thing I ask. The motive, according to John, is my "full joy". Why would I not make my joy a measure and a specific part of my praying? Often, incidentally, I will not ask for certain things, usually requested by someone else, because there is no joy for me in the answer. If Aunt Sue's neighbor's friend's niece's co-worker at the Beauty Shop's bunions will bring you joy—then pray like there's no tomorrow. I just can't find the joy in it today.

So why do we not see more joyful answers? James tells us unmistakably,

> *Yet you do not have because you do not ask. You ask and do not receive, because you ask amiss, that you may spend it on your pleasures. (James 4:2-3)*

We do not have because we do not ask. This is our Lord's point exactly in John 16. We do not have because we ask wrongly. Here James tells us that selfish, self-spent motives are the death-knell for answered prayer.

I take it that the two are related. Not only does true selfish motive take us away from God and His glory, but fulfilling our selfish desires does not bring us joy. Have you not noticed, when you get something you crave, that the desire is satisfied for a while. For a while this is true, and then sure as the rising of the moon, a new craving sets on, and in, until you are pulled to fulfill it all over again.

Not so joy. Not so the profound and resonant thrill of seeing the wonder of God answering prayer. This prayer, when fulfilled, is often an answer for others;

and if not, it is an answer that moves you to want more of Him, not simply, more answers.

How about you and prayer? James states for us the relationship between having and asking. If motives are clear and joy is in view, then all that remains is to ask. Asking by its nature, means specifics. Specifically, exactly, directly ask God for His answer. Ask Him for a "yes". Quit guarding everything and trying to cover for God. Say it specifically so that when He says, "Yes," it will be an unmistakable and unquestionable answer from Him. Say it exactly so that you can have joy and bring Him delight, knowing He really did answer your prayer just as you asked. This is the kind of prayer God responds to for His glory and according to His way. The truth is that vague prayer is tantamount to not asking. How might my prayer and this chapter have been changed or destroyed by a vague prayer? My foot on the first step in perfect unison with the vans' arrival made it a magical, mystical, and joyful moment. What moments await you when you cast aside vague joyless prayers for the simple lesson God underscored for me in Uganda?

God Tends To Answer Prayer
As Specifically As You Ask

VI

YOU CAN ASK AND RECEIVE A GREATER MEASURE OF WHAT YOU NEED FOR YOUR GIFT

This lesson is more personal than practical. My assumption, perhaps my conviction, is that what I've begun to experience regarding my gift will hold true for you and your gift. You should relate if you have a talent that you aren't very fond of.

Specifically, I wrote in my notebook the following:

I have asked and am receiving greater and greater measures of earnestness for my preaching.

Perhaps my story here will encourage you or perhaps it will encourage your pastor or someone just entering the ministry. Along with Charles Finney, I too believe that an energized and extemporaneous pulpit could do much to turn the tide for the gospel of grace in our times.

Energized and extemporaneous may be unfamiliar terms, so let me explain. Many years ago when I began to preach/teach as a professional effort, I was haunted by the words of one of my professors. He observed to us as fledgling movers-and-shakers in Christ, that "you can impress from a distance, but you impact face-to-face." He meant that disciple-making really occurs in close contact with people. I desired, and still desire, to touch lives with God's Word. He said it happens up close, so I took it to heart.

My first job in a church was to serve as an Associate Pastor over evangelism and discipleship. We developed discipleship materials that continue to bear fruit and are being used in both America and Uganda. For me, disciple-making was the thing and I was hard at work trying to organize the church's efforts to make disciples. Small groups, special training, one-on-one materials, all suited our hope of building people up in Christ.

Suddenly, however, a problem appeared. The Pastor resigned, most of the church left, and I agreed to stay on through a "transition". The transition has lasted sixteen years; none of which I'd sign up for again, and none of which I'd trade for anything.

During the transition I was given the responsibility to occupy the pulpit during the Sunday morning worship service. I had been trained for this and tried to faithfully teach God's Word (I spent my first two years on the book of Ephesians!). I only had one little problem; I hated preaching. My original agreement when hired included an understanding that I would rarely be in the pulpit. After all, we impact face-to-face!

I really did loath preaching. I wouldn't even call it by its name. I called it "teaching". Every week I was obligated to labor in the passage for hours and hours to finally come to an exegetical solution. Of course, the commentaries were very important to pour over, which I did as a discipline—though most of them, being in the critical tradition tell you what a passage doesn't mean rather than what it does mean. Following this effort, I dutifully converted the exegetical material (An instructional letter to the Ephesians regarding their calling...) into a homiletical form (We are called by God...). After getting the outline into a good form, illustrations, introductions, and conclusions had to be added. Finally, and my "favorite" part, practice it until you can deliver it with freshness!

Every Sunday, for years, I would go home and sleep for about two hours from exhaustion. My greatest hope was that God would minister grace to the audience. My greatest goal was to get it over with.

All of this began to change as I wrestled with one glaring problem; people seemed appreciative and impacted by my messages. So a genuine quandary appeared. "Why would I be given an ability by God and hate it?" I continued to wonder about this dilemma, focusing always on disciple-making, whether in the form of counseling, leading, or more formally discipling.

One day, however, it struck me. I was stunned and the truth glared at me.

Gifts are exceptions. It was certainly true that we impact face-to-face, but it isn't all that is true. A true preacher, as I discovered, is called and equipped by God to impact in an unusual way. A preacher impacts from a distance through his words, and later I'd discover, through his personality.

All of this set me on a new course to discover how to be faithful, yes, and enjoy the very activity God had called me to. During these moments of clarification God led me to the writings of two men from the past; Phillips Brooks and Charles Spurgeon. Spurgeon, who ministered in England, is the most famous of the two, and remains the most prolific and widely read preacher and writer in history. Brooks was the American version of Spurgeon and is most famed for his Christmas carol, 'O Little Town of Bethlehem'. The impact of these men on my life was so pronounced that I named my last child after them. Formally he is Charles Haddon Brooks Lybrand. Informally, we call him Brooks.

Earnestness, zeal, energy, and personality are seasoned through their works. Here are a few passages I have come to cherish.

> *Preaching is the communication of truth by man to men... [It] is the bringing of truth through the personality*[2]

---

[2] Phillip Brooks, <u>The Joy of Preaching</u>, (Grand Rapids: Kregel Publications, 1989), p. 9.

Let a man be a true preacher, really uttering the truth through his own personality, and it is strange how men will gather to listen to him.[3]

If I am right in this idea, then it will follow that the preacher's life must be a life of large accumulation. He must not be always trying to make sermons, but always seeking truth, and out of the truth which he has won the sermons will make themselves.[4]

On the other hand, the extemporaneous discourse has the advantage of alertness. It gives a sense of liveliness. It is more immediately striking. It possesses more activity and warmth. It conveys an idea of steadiness and readiness, of poise and self-possession, even to the most rude perceptions. Men have an admiration for it, as indicating a mastery of powers and an independence of artificial helps...Add to these merely that the proportion of extemporaneous preaching may well be increased as a man grows older in the ministry...[5]

Let your own nature freely shape its own ways. Only be sure that those ways do really come out of your nature, and not out of the merely accidental circumstances of your first parish.[6]

---

[3] Ibid, p. 29.
[4] Ibid, p. 122.
[5] Ibid, pp. 129-130.
[6] Ibid, p. 87.

I gave you a golden rule for securing attention at the commencement, namely, always say something worth hearing; I will now give you a diamond rule, and conclude. Be yourself clothed with the Spirit of God, and then no question about attention or non-attention will arise.[7]

Good impromptu speech is just the utterance of a practiced thinker— a man of information, meditating on his legs, and allowing his thoughts to march through his mouth into the open air. Think aloud as much as you can when you are alone, and you will soon be on the high road to success in this matter.[8]

If I were asked— What in a Christian minister is the most essential quality for securing success... I should reply, "earnestness": and if I were asked a second or a third time, I should not vary the answer.[9]

It is not in the order of nature that rivers should run uphill, and it does not often happen that zeal rises from the pew to the pulpit. It is natural that it should flow down from us to our hearers; the pulpit must

[7] Charles H. Spurgeon, <u>Lectures To My Students</u>, Ministries Resources Library, (Grand Rapids: Zondervan, 1954), p. 139.
[8] Ibid, p. 149.
[9] Charles H. Spurgeon, <u>Lectures To My Students</u>, Ministries Resources Library, (Grand Rapids: Zondervan, 1954), p. 305.

therefore stand at a high level of ardour, if we are, under God, to make and keep our people fervent.[10]

At this same time, as I was coming to conclusions about the preaching gift, Dr. Earl Radmacher came to our church to teach a Spiritual Gifts seminar[11]. His definition of "preaching" was both a clarification and confirmation to me:

Preaching is the God-given ability to set before people the Word and wisdom of God persuasively through personality as a herald.

That was it. The combination of insights made it clear. I would begin to preach in a style unique to me and my design by God. My first warning to the congregation was a sermon in which I likened my own struggles to the biblical problem of David wearing Saul's armor. Imagine the tragedy if David had faced the giant in an oversized, stiff armored jacket! Instead, he did what he knew to do; he did what he was made to do...unto the Lord. I began studying hard, reflecting deeply, and sharing extemporaneously; forming the words in the moment as I explained the passage or truth in the way which seemed best to me as I depended on God's Spirit and His providence.

---

[10] Ibid, p. 306.

[11] A video tape series of Dr. Radmacher's teaching on Spiritual Gifts is available by contacting Dr. Radmacher at drr10@juno.com, or 3417 Lake Vanessa Cir. NW, Salem, OR 97304.

It wasn't great at first, and it may not be great now; however, especially since Uganda, people consistently, month-in and month-out, tell me how much growth they see in my communication. They also tell me how they are actually applying what I'm sharing with them from the Word of God. Recently I received the best encouragement, "You stretch us."

So what happened in Uganda? On the flight I read Dallimore's biography on George Whitefield, the great evangelist of the colonial period. I was again struck with how important earnestness is to the preacher. Indeed, this one thing seemed to be my greatest drawback. I know a fire in my soul, but display a sheltered candle. I flicker in my communication compared to the fire-flash I have to offer. So what happened? I prayed. I prayed very specifically. I asked the Lord for more earnestness.

My asking could be inappropriate, and I realized it as I prayed. Romans 12:3 states that we have each been given a "measure of faith". I take it that Paul is specifically referring to a limit on the amount or capability of the gift we've been given at our spiritual birth (1 Corinthians 12:11). The context for our "measure of faith" is the gifts of the Spirit, therefore it stands to reason that we each have been given a limit within which to serve the Lord by serving others. This "measure" would also explain why gifted individuals have different extents of their ministries. Billy Graham, Billy Sunday, Bill Bright, and every other Bill can have faithful ministries with varying results. On the one hand, each of us can vary in our faithfulness; but on the other hand, we can vary in the "measure of faith" God has given.

You can see why my asking might be wrong; however, consider an additional point. I wasn't asking for a greater gift, but simply for my gift to be more fully realized. I wanted the earnestness in my heart to match the earnestness in my voice and words.

In a way I wanted more grace. Not more of a gift, but more of the gift He had given and I continued to hide. Listen to Peter's words,

> ...and be clothed with humility, for
> "God resists the proud,
> But gives grace to the humble."
> Therefore humble yourselves under the mighty hand of God, that He may exalt you in due time... (1 Peter 5:5-6)

Since this passage is written to individuals who had already trusted in Christ, it can only mean that the believer who humbles himself can receive even more grace from God. I had decided to humble myself by refusing to insist on having several gifts, by refusing to have a greater measure than I had. I had humbled myself by accepting God's will from my heart; and now, all I wanted was to be as fully faithful with my earnestness, my energy, my burn for the truth, that I asked God to give me all that He has for me within my gift. He answered my prayer.

In the course of my time in Uganda the Lord placed in front of me two important individuals. Morris

Ogenga, the visionary leader of the efforts in his nation; and Jehoshaphat Wanyama, a zealous and knowledgeable pastor in one of the churches we've planted.

Jehoshaphat spent a day in ministry with me in which we, together, saw hundreds of students respond to the gospel of grace. After our ministry together, he asked if we could continue our conversation about a point of theology. I invited him to join me on the grounds of the hotel and we shared coffee and a Coke, with fellowship I have seldom known. This man, Jehoshaphat, was a man of heart and zeal, and I learned that day of the sacrifices with his family, his career, and his heritage he had made. I was awed, inspired, and freed to sell out a little more for the Lord and preach with the zeal I saw inside and outside Jehoshaphat. He told me, late in our conversation, how much he had learned that day from me about preaching the Word. I still do not know what he learned, but that moment was no time for a competition of gratitude between new friends and coworkers in Christ.

Your gift may not be preaching, but it is your gift. Consider, perhaps for the first time, Peter's words,

> As each one has received a gift, minister it to one another, as good stewards of the manifold grace of God. (1 Peter 4:10)

God is calling you to serve fully with it, even if you don't exactly know what "it" is. He is calling you and He will make the path known. Don't be afraid to ask Him for what you need for your gift. Also, don't be afraid to ask Him specifically.

You Can Ask And Receive A Greater Measure Of What You Need For Your Gift

VII

ALL PEOPLE ARE THE SAME...CULTURE ONLY PUTS A SPIN ON THE SAMENESS

Again, he milks a cow, his cow, as a matter of routine. The cow, the corn, the vegetables, the wife inside at work, the children run about; life is as it should be, or life is as it is—both mean the same thing to the man who repeats each day. He works hard because he does what he has to; then two men arrive, one is from America, the other is someone his wife knows from church. Yes, she attends church, and though the walk is many miles she attends regularly, a Bible study, too; but he works because it is the way life is. The two men sit in the chairs and the man apologizes as he must finish milking, but they are patient and he is patient...much as the whole land of Uganda is patient.

Wars, dictators, rabid and radical fundamentalists of all kinds have killed, maimed, and beaten the people of Uganda. Disease has been a relentless enemy as well, and the strange notion promoted by the shaman, or witch doctor, calls for sex with a virgin to cure AIDS. Many young girls are raped and the disease spreads along with moral violation of young and innocent children. Also, there is circumcision, a ceremonial rite to manhood, performed with a knife used from man to man, and more AIDS and pestilence spreads. People do not often live long in Uganda, and the country has lost its infra-structure and its way, because no one can remember the lessons needed to pass on to each generation about life, and business, and wisdom.

Ugandans know of war and suffering and the weather which turns against them too by giving clouds, but no water, and famine adds to the stuck ways and the stymied world.

So this man works because now he owns his land and Uganda is democratic and a Christian is now the president. Changes are afoot and Uganda is honored as the example in Africa for combating AIDS. Uganda is winning many battles in the two-steps-forward-one-step-backwards way progress is made in the Third World, maybe any world, when the truth is honestly seen; unaltered by the politicians, the media, or our own unstudied opinions about the way the world is.

The man sits and the American opens the Word of God. The man has talked with many missionaries, rejecting each plea for his soul, but his wife sews in the doorway peering at the three men with occasional smiles as she prays, and her husband with his back to her, answers the questions in a different way than before. She has prayed to the Lord because she is a believer, and wants her husband to know and share the Lord with her. It is important and she knows it in her heart, and maybe her head, looking at a man who has worked hard to produce all that is about them: a sturdy home with the luxury of tin for the roof, a small silo for storage as something few have, with a cow, with a garden, with chickens, with so much, but a husband who does not have God or know God.

Just then a cock shoots from the window and flies directly at the face of the American who ducks and laughs and continues with the Word of God. She still sits in the doorway and smiles in a way that looks like crying. He wants to trust in Christ and she is thrilled, but restrained and quiet as a Ugandan woman. The message made it to the man this time, or perhaps, the message was different. It was about grace and faith and how the works meant much to his family and his country...but the works mean nothing to God, and the man knew it all along, but only now did the American and the man from his wife's church show him God's invitation to become a God-child by faith and not by the works that others praise. The man knows his life, his routine, his works took away none of the darkness in his heart. He prayed sincerely with the men. A new church and a new relationship with the Lord, altogether as a family, now meant this family could grow and offer a new part to a new future for their village and their nation. She beamed and the men walked away leaving her literature to study, and taking with them the names and address for the new pastor of the new church to come visit soon. They want this visit, and this church, and the husband and wife and children have a new future in this life begun...and a new future in the next life assured.

I was the American and this happened on June 17, 2001. It wasn't just this event, but certainly this event, that underscored for me the much needed shattering of my misconceptions. I've lived in America my entire life and the images of ignorance and darkness hung over my head as unwanted assumptions, unwanted clouds that threatened a downpour of continued prejudice...no, arrogance is a better word.

In Uganda I found what I find daily in America. I see wives who pray and hope for their hard working husbands to come to know Christ and take some role in providing spiritual leadership for the family, the children, the community in which they live. I find educated people in Uganda who read and write in two or three languages, and who know their Bible and debate theology.

In Uganda I find parents saving money and sacrificing to send their children to school, because they believe school, education, is a way, or the way, to give a new future to their babies. They want their children to succeed beyond themselves; and isn't this America too? What do you want for your kids, and wouldn't you travel a long distance to see the best medical help available, no matter the cost, when a disease strikes your child? Ugandans are the same.

Point after point after point: Ugandans are the same. They have alcoholics, and babies, and death. They read the papers, they discuss the issues, some seek to know God, and some seek to divert people into falsehood and error. They are just like you and the man or woman on TV you hate the most. They are human beings in need of grace and truth. In the election year they were for George W. Bush and hoped he would win the election, and he did, and they were happy.

When the towers fell they cried or laughed, depending...And in all of this they often make the same mistake. They think we are different and that Americans possess something better than they do. Everyone, including us, including them, including the best theorist and socio-cultural researchers are wrong. The nature of man and woman and child is fundamentally and essentially the same. Culture is a dress and spin that Rousseau tried to fool us with; but died as he lived, in stark-raving error concerning the explanation of human behavior due to society rather than nature.

Of course, there are differences. Our toilets are off the floor while theirs in the villages are flush with the ground. Our women show their knees, while Ugandan women wouldn't dare. Our women nurse their babies with discretion, while Ugandan women nurse their babies with open necessity... and what of these things? Are they manners or innovations or superstitions?

Genuinely ask yourself, "So what?" Why do these cultural anomalies and idiosyncrasies make any difference at all? Are they superstitions? We can read our horoscopes daily, employ a pet clairvoyant, and watch a man with two first names talk to the dead on television. You think we're different? The truth is we are not different. We just like our culture more than theirs. We like our culture in the same way we like our old jeans.

All People Are The Same...Culture Only Puts A Spin On The Sameness

Consider... women and men and children and families and government and death and play and work ...and God. It is the same trying existence which we all live. We look for purpose and joy and fulfillment and a way, some way, to not die, to not leave our children worse off, and to not ignore the profound spiritual longings of our hearts.

Today you can quit playing the political pundit— spinning your life as unique, different, better or worse than the wealthy or poor in your town, the democratic or republican in your country, the black or white, educated or ignorant, in our world.

Yes, there is evil. Yes, there are enemies. Today, however, by God's mercy you can stop, forever, the silly and flawed notions you have about differences. We aren't different; we just live out cultural spins, thinking all the while there is right and wrong here—your way, naturally, being right. This lesson, maybe above them all, is the great chain on American Christianity. When we drop this chain, as it has no padlock, we can step forward in Christian grace, love, truth, and impact. We, I predict, will also see evil with precision, just as Paul invited us to do two thousand years ago.

For we do not wrestle against flesh and blood, but against principalities, against powers, against the rulers of the darkness of this age, against spiritual hosts of wickedness in the heavenly place. (Ephesians 6:13)

All People Are The Same...Culture Only Puts A Spin On The Sameness

VIII

LIMITS YIELD INTENSITY

Limits yield intensity.[12] What an odd little phrase this is, that limits yield intensity. Of course, in it is the great explanation for how those who focus, really focus; and for how such contrived epidemics as Attention Deficit Disorder (or ADHD) can be cured for good in any person. It also explains a lot of what we saw in Uganda.

Everything we experienced in Uganda involved the magnitude and the power of this simple observation: Limits yield intensity. I first encountered this insight in Williamston, Vermont, during a week-long training on the creative process led by Robert and Rosalind Fritz.

"This afternoon bring a sack of stuff to the session," Robert instructed us. "What kind of stuff?" I

---

[12]If you would like to read some further thinking on this phrase and *The Power of Limits*, see Stephen Nachmanovitch's book, <u>Free Play</u>, (New York: Jeremy P. Tarcher/Putnam, 1990), pp. 78-93.

or someone asked. "Anything," he said a little fiendishly. During the break after lunch I gathered twigs, paper clips, sunglasses, etc. Little did I know this would be an answer to my prayer at the beginning of the week during the long trek on Southwest Airlines. I had prayed specifically, "Lord, teach me how to focus."

For as long as I can remember, I have been in a state of constant interruption. I've been known to interrupt myself interrupting someone else...and don't miss the point; I don't want to be changed. My design is from God and I can show you as many advantages as you can show me disadvantages for my talent.

Indeed, one of the most trying issues of parenthood is making the distinction between character and talents in our children. A distractible child like me is often the same child you don't want to debate when he's grown, since his talent for taking multiple and parallel arguments to his combatant is a talent few can withstand (I've secretly always longed to be on a show like "Crossfire"). These distractible children grow up to become patently brilliant in a crisis or an emergency room. The last thing we need are "uninterruptible" emergency room physicians who tell the patient with a flooding jugular, "You'll just have to wait until I'm through wrapping this sprained ankle."

That child who wiggles and wiggles may be the same hero who climbs a ladder, flight of stairs, or mountain to rescue you. Discipline is one thing, and a very important thing. However, trying to discipline the talents out of a person is a bit of foolishness we might as well lay to rest.

So, I'm interruptible and I want to focus; do these contradict? Not if I can learn how to engage either when needed or desired.

Robert had us move all of the chairs out of the way and gave us a large sheet of blank white paper to accompany our gathered "stuff". The exercise was simple. We were creating "ensembles", a picture or artwork made of stuff arranged on the paper. The process was simple. Look at the stuff, look at the blank page, look at the stuff, look at the blank page, imagine your artwork/picture/creation, and...Go! You have two minutes! "Wow, two minutes," I panicked as I began to work with my stuff. At that moment an amazing thing happened to me, the entire world went timeless and irrelevant. I assume I felt like Einstein did when at age 16, he imagined riding on a beam of light and peering into a mirror to the side to see if he saw his reflection (he did, incidentally, and this whole e=mc^2 thing was set in motion).

I was timeless in that I felt suddenly as though I had all day to form my ensemble. With each action and each adjustment I noticed, in all my overwhelming focus, that the entire noisy and busy room around me didn't mean a thing. There was no need to move away or "hush" anyone. I was in a zone of experience that I've learned to repeat over and over again.

I remember this same frame of focused intensity the day God permitted me to revive a blue and water-filled six year-old named Kenny. Dozens of people were all around, no doubt making noise, if only gasps. I heard no one. The paramedics were on the way and I prayed silently, "I hope this works - Lord save this child." I breathed in...water came out...I breathed in...water came out, and a slight gasp. Another small breath, and another, and his eyes flickered. He lived with no damage to his brain or life. During those moments I felt there was time, no distractions, nothing except a pure focus on the next step of giving my air to that boy. Have you ever noticed how LIMITS YIELD INTENSITY?

The point is profound. In "summer physics" most children discover that a nozzle or a thumb over the end of a garden hose causes the water to spray with more force and greater distance. Simply put, a nozzle puts a greater limit on the space available for the water to leave the hose. This limited space causes a greater intensity in the form of a narrow stream of water to occur.

As I encountered a drowning boy, the deadline, or limit of impending death caused a great focus on my part to take specific and measured steps to bring an exiting life back to us.

Two minutes, the stuff available, and a picture in my mind, created an intense focus. The time, items, and picture limited all my options, which then yielded an intensity of focus. The principle is solid, LIMITS YIELD INTENSITY.

Stephen Nachmanovitch adds, "One rule I have found to be useful is that *two rules is more than enough.*"[13] You'll find successful leaders, businessmen, parents, and

---

[13] Stephen Nachmanovitch, <u>Free Play</u>, (New York: Jeremy P. Tarcher/Putnam, 1990), p. 83.

57

artists all learn to simplify by limiting the "rules" they follow, and the principles they employ, to a very few...but an important few.

⸻⸻⸻⸻⸻

So what of Uganda? Perhaps no lesson loomed bigger to me than this one. In fact, it helps explain so much of what we experienced in Uganda, that I placed it here, at the beginning of the lessons.

Uganda was a short-term missions trip. Short-term means there was a specific limit to the event. A leave date, a return date, an "open the new church date", and a "begin to share the gospel from hut-to-hut date". All of these dates served as limits, which in turn, produced focus.

The limits didn't stop there. The time to travel from hut-to-hut, or from school-to-school was a limit. The priority of being back at the hotel by dark for safety and rest was a limit. The necessity of using a translator was a limit. The limits, though numerous, actually were few and specific, compared to what might have been "limitless". Imagine if we had no return date. Many missionaries live without that limit; therefore they are sometimes unfocused unless other limits are established. Without a return date we might have casually "explored" Uganda before "getting down to business". Without a specific village (Namaje, pronounce Nah-mah-jay) we might have wandered through Uganda sharing the gospel sporadically and randomly with whomever we encountered.

Can you see the power of LIMITS YIELD INTENSITY? Given our limits in Uganda what would this principle predict about our intensity, our focus? We were intense! Using a translator and limiting the conversation to explaining and offering the gospel, creates a focus on the words and inflection chosen. Limiting the time to cover a village section creates a focused move to the next place. The same holds true for traveling and speaking at a limited number of schools in one day, or what must be accomplished by nightfall at a crusade.

Even as I describe all we did, I am dizzied by the memories. However, we were simply focused at the time, and the intense experience was exhilarating and timeless; not unlike the experiences with the ensemble or Kenny.

In Psalm 90, when the Lord directs us to "number our days", isn't this a limit, designed by God, to create a focus for our short lives towards eternity? Haven't we all observed the temptation of youth to assume immortality on earth leading them to fritter away their time and lives?

What about you? Do you find little intensity and even less focus in your job, ministry, or day-to-day life? Could it be that you have violated the principle of LIMITS YIELD INTENSITY? Is your lack of motivation, or focus, or zest for your day-to-day life victimized by the lack of limits?

There can be many causes for exhaustion, depression, and diminished motivation. Few things, however, can overcome a diffused spirit. When we conclude we can do anything and have all the time in the world in which to do it; no focus, no intensity can arise. God designed His universe this way. Christ Himself was focused, due especially to His limited objectives, audiences, and time frame. He accomplished everything, right on schedule; even to die well for us.

What, and in the right moment, could this lesson mean to you? What two or three commitments could you limit yourself to this week? What time deadline could you add to that project haunting you everyday? If you want focus and intensity, create limits...limits of any kind. The moment you determine a limit, you invite the very design of God's created order to come to your aid. Look what He did in six days!

Finally, perhaps as an aside, LIMITS YIELD INTENSITY finds one of its greatest applications in the marriage relationship. When we limit our love, tenderness, and care to one other human being, the great possibility of intense and focused intimacy is born. How might the addition of limits in your relationships transform them? You can only know by an honest effort. Enjoy!

Limits Yield Intensity

IX

CHRISTIANITY CAN BE LIVED EVERY MOMENT

One day at Dallas Seminary, David asked me a simple question, or rather posed a logical riddle. David is the son of a theologian of some renown, so questions from David were the norm. Questions in seminary were the norm as well, but this question and answer session has stayed with me all these years.

"Is it possible not to sin at any given moment?" David began.

"Yes," I said.

"Is it possible not to sin at every given moment?" he continued.

"No," I replied. "It is not possible to not sin at every given moment." David was considering the possibility that Christians can live sinless lives; a premise the Bible flatly rejects.

"Why not?" he asked. "Ought implies can [meaning that if we should never sin, then we are able to never sin by God's design], and if we can not sin at any given moment, then we can not sin at every given moment!"

As I write these words I thankfully notice that I'm no longer in seminary, though I miss David and many other friends.

"David," I said. "Can you be awake at any given moment?"

"Yes," he said.

"Can you be awake at every given moment?" He was silent so I politely said, "No. You cannot be awake at every given moment. Eventually the principle or need for sleep will override the effort to stay awake."

David then looked at me and said, "That's what my dad believes."

I haven't seen David since those days, and I'm sure he has things sorted out, while still asking lots of great questions. I've always appreciated what discussions with David meant to my own growth.

That conversation helped me as I studied my Bible, to conclude that God's expectation for His children is not the ideal we assume. God does not expect us to never sin in this life.

Already I can imagine someone reading this with a ready argument. Please hold on as we think this through. Few insights have meant more to my personal sanity than this one: *God does not expect his children to never sin in this life.*

"Never sinning" is an ideal. Ideals are impossible and non-existent. Therefore, if God expects an ideal from us, He expects the impossible.

Dan Sullivan, of The Strategic Coach, offers a helpful illustration in his talks. He asks his audience to define the "horizon". Of course, the horizon is the line where the earth meets the sky. Even though most of us know this definition, few of us have stopped to notice that the horizon doesn't actually exist. The earth never meets the sky! Dan goes on to explain how ideals, in time, tend to discourage us if we keep measuring our progress by them. You can walk toward the horizon all day, and at the end, you'll be no closer to it than your first step!

Too many Christians and too many Christian leaders impose ideals on the Christian life. Ideals, like the horizon, are fine to organize our decisions concerning where we're headed next; but they are never a useful measure of our progress in the faith.

Let me lay it to rest. In this life, Christianity can be defined as "stumbling in the right direction". John tells us in his first epistle,

> *If we say that we have no sin, we deceive ourselves, and the Truth is not in us. (1 John 1:8)*

I, along with many others, believe this is a reference to our retained nature of sin. However, the laws of cause-and-effect being what they are, a bent to sin will show up as acts of sin. Shocking as it may seem, sinning (stumbling) is a part of living the Christian life; just as falling is a part of learning to walk. Few of us berate our toddlers for falling down while they're learning to walk. Why do we berate fellow Christians, or even ourselves, for the exact same thing spiritually? Of course, as we mature we physically and spiritually fall less often and less severely. But please take note: falling is always a genuine possibility, and will happen, so long as we live in a world with the physical and spiritual laws we have.

Just because you can walk-and-not-fall at any given moment, there is no guarantee that you will walk-and-not-fall at every given moment. John anticipated this fact for us in the verse before the one mentioned:

> But if we walk in the light as He is in the light, we have fellowship with one another, and the blood of Jesus Christ His Son cleanses us from all sin. (1 John 1:7)

An honest look at the verse reveals two simple facts. First, we are able to walk in the light of Christ. To "walk in the light" is to not "walk in the darkness". Walking in the light carries with it all the good things a Christian hopes. It is a walk in fellowship with the Lord. It is a walk in displayed love for others. It is a walk with a clear conscience and openly good choices and actions. It is a walk in the light with Jesus Christ. The second thing of note in this verse is that His blood cleanses us from all sin. Please notice this particular cleansing from sin occurs *while we walk in the light* and not beforehand. Also, we're cleansed from ALL sin. Now honestly, if we can walk in the light and still need to be continually cleansed, doesn't it insist that "sinning" is involved in (as a part of) walking in the light? Of course. Living genuine Christianity is stumbling in the right direction. It is not living an ideal. Christianity is possible in its biblical form, but impossible as the current ideal many attempt to demand you attain.

The conversation about ideals here is very relevant to Uganda and the lesson taught by the trip: *Christianity can be lived every moment.*

We fondly call it Uganda time. It's the reason we sit and wait in front of the hotel. Naturally, as Americans, we're keeping to the schedule. We've washed, eaten breakfast, had a meeting, sung to God's glory, and prayed for the day. But now, there are no vans. No vans means we can't get to our village of Namaje. If we're not in our village we can't be about our work...so we wait. This waiting, however, is very different from our waiting in America. As I look at the team, they are scattered about in different activities while waiting. Many, especially the women I've known for years, have taken out their Bibles and are reading. It is not the reading of study or of wrestling with a theological question; instead it is the reading the heart does when the mind is not dragging the person away to the next thing. These ladies are softly and quietly making full use of the moment to saturate their hearts in preparation for the day ahead – if the day happens – on Uganda time. Others are writing in journals, some are encouraging those needing encouragement due to some fear or ill-ease brought on by the food or travel. The remainder of the team is involved in clarifying details, as team leaders tend to do, or sharing our story and message with an interested hotel guest.

The surprising thing is that it all seems patiently organized. Perhaps it's the time constraints, or the purpose, or the nature of these events; however, I can only conclude that it is the faith these people are all wearing so openly. Since we are missionaries, albeit short-term, we are all focused on the mission. The mission itself works to organize our thinking to stay clear of everything which does not contribute to the mission. Taking the gift of free moments to bolster our hearts makes sense; in fact, it is the most natural thing for us to do since we are living our Christianity moment to moment.

Why, when people return from such an experience do they return to a life unfrequented by a vibrant faith? Certainly "limits yield intensity", but it is more than that. I believe it is fundamentally caused by a memory lapse, or perhaps, a decision lapse. When we arrive in a foreign land with a specific purpose, our behavior is invited, even demanded, to represent our nation and our faith well. Why should anything change in our day-to-day life when we come home? Consider the words from the author of Hebrews,

> For here we have no continuing city but we seek the one to come. (Hebrews 13:14)

The truth is that our lives in our own earthly nation are no different than our speedy trip to Uganda.

At the very best, our lives on earth are a whisper, a vapor, a fading flower. It's for a time, a very short time. We who know the Savior have been invited to represent and serve Him well. Why would a wait in a doctor's office be any different than the wait on the steps of the Mt. Elgon Hotel in Uganda?

Uganda brought in glaring splendor, the fact that Christianity can be lived at every moment. We watched it and lived it. It is not like sleep or sin, since it is God's desire that we live our faith at all times. A foolish definition that idealizes Christianity won't get us there. Nor will a casual decision to walk with God as best we can (usually on Sunday mornings and in a major crisis). Rather, God is inviting each of us to walk with Him, and before Him, as a way of life. Christianity can be lived on vacation, while you sleep, while you are intimate with your spouse, while you change a diaper, and while you cry at the loss of a parent. Primarily it comes down to a fundamental choice concerning your entire life and its being entrusted to God. Second, it involves a consistent focus on all that contributes to a moment-by-moment Christianity. Two verses are near and dear on this lesson. Consider them well:

> I beseech you therefore, brethren, by the mercies of God, that you present your bodies a living sacrifice, holy, acceptable to God, which is your reasonable service. And do not be conformed to this world, but be transformed by the renewing of your mind, that you may prove what is that good and acceptable and perfect will of God.

(Romans 12:1-2)

Finally, brethren, whatever things are true, whatever things are noble, whatever things are just, whatever things are pure, whatever things are lovely, whatever things are of good report, if there is any virtue and if there is anything praiseworthy – meditate on these things. (Philippians 4:8)

Christianity Can Be Lived Every Moment

X

SUCCESS ELSEWHERE TEMPTS US TO UNFAIRLY CRITICIZE HOME, WHEN THE REAL POINT IS...

The very first time I felt it was when he sat across from me eating picante sauce and chips. We were neither friends nor enemies at the time, just new acquaintances talking about the things we loved. I really had no defense. I didn't even have anything to defend. He was a missionary, at least one on the way. He was off to a foreign field for what I felt he painted as the glory of true labor in the Lord. He spoke of America and all the problems she had; that is, all the problems besetting the Church in America.

We are lazy. We are spoiled. We care nothing for the lost. We are ravaged by spiritual diseases that keep us weak and sick and incapable of being faithful to the high calling and forthright opportunities God has handed us.

So many blessings came to me as I shared this meal in a now absent El Chico restaurant. El Chico, "The Boy"; what a perfect bit of symbolism on God's providential part. I was indeed a boy and my boyish views snapped into shape that day. "Why is he so critical?" I wondered to myself. As the days turned into weeks I continued to wrestle over all he had said. Now to his credit, he was simply sharing his views from a missionary's perspective; which is a very difficult thing to grasp without going to the foreign field.

Before we continue, may I ask you a question? As a Christian, are you interested in foreign missions? If you do not know Christ, then of course you are understandably excused. How could one who has not yet tasted the grace and mercy of God be expected to have any desire to bring the free offer of the gospel to those who haven't heard?

If you know the Lord and missions doesn't interest you, don't you think something's amiss? Given the wonder of the gift, why wouldn't you want others to hear?

The first time I had an inkling of the criticism against American Christianity was the day a visiting speaker, who incidentally was headed to the Pacific Ocean and beyond to serve God, spoke to our (then) small church. This particular man came and spoke to a church that had been recently decimated by the cycle of conflict and departure most American churches experience from time to time. The people who remained, although battered and bruised, listened intently as this man explained the great problem with the American Church: "koinonitus". The disease is a take-off on the Greek word for "fellowship" found throughout the New Testament. His critique was that American Christianity fellowships too much, is too inwardly focused, and consequently, doesn't care about evangelism or sharing the gospel with the lost. Our church, sad to say, needed "koinonitus". We needed to re-establish a true community.

I had an inkling of the problem at first, and clear understanding some time later. Why the criticism? The criticism comes from a simple assumption: *Spirituality is determined by results.*

Actually, that's all there is to it. Americans are profoundly pragmatic, which is why marketing phrases such as "it worked for me" are so compelling. Success is spirituality. Success is the blessing of God. With this mindset, it is no wonder we are busy counting and collecting anecdotes and examples. We want to get in on the move of God. Many teachers, in fact, advise us to find out what God is doing, track it down, and join in.

Doesn't this mentality create the faddish nature of our Christianity? Programs, models, strategies, tactics, experiences, encounters, etc., flood our lives because we want to be successful. Our success, however, has an underlying motivation: we want to be spiritual.

Nothing is wrong with wanting to be spiritual, or with desiring success. However, when we have a false equation operating in our heads, we can make serious, though understandable mistakes. Spirituality does not necessarily mean success, nor does success necessarily mean one is spiritual.

Do you remember the truth tables from Logic 101? Robert Fritz has invented a new kind of logic table which shows all of the options available, in this instance, between two separate elements. It looks like this:

Element A				
Element B				

The elements can relate to each other in four possible ways, illustrated below.

Element A	+	+	−	−
Element B	+	−	+	−

The value of this kind of truth table is, literally, for us to see the truth. Take for example, parenting. Good parents and good children have a relationship. Many people mistakenly believe this incomplete version of the relationship between parenting and how children "turn out".

Good Parents	+			−
Good Children	+			−

In this version good parents lead to good children, or "good children" prove "good parents". By the same reasoning, if you see bad children (bottom right box), what would you conclude about the parents (top right box)? All you can conclude is that they are bad parents (the negative of good parents).

What's wrong with this logic? The middle two options are missing. Here's the complete chart:

Good Parents	+	+	–	–
Good Children	+	–	+	–

Now we see all of the options. Good parents can have good children. Bad parents can have bad children. However, good parents can also have bad children, and bad parents also can have good children. Don't you know of someone who turned out well despite their parents or home environment? Maybe it was you!

All of these options are valid or possible. If you'd like to see biblical proof, Ezekiel 18 spells it out in irrefutable detail. Humans have a will with which they make choices. God's grace reaches beyond "bad influences" to often reclaim a wayward soul. The quality of parents does not dictate the quality of the individual. Each will stand or fall on his own. So, how would you bet? I'd bet on good parents producing good kids, but I'm going with the tendency without demanding a guarantee.

Now, what about the issue of success and spirituality? Well, consider Fritz's truth table.

Spirituality	+			–
Success	+			–

In this example, which is the way many people tend to think, success and being truly spiritual are incompletely related. This incomplete thinking is why they assume a "lack of success" in the church means a lack of spirituality. Success, in our example, means evangelistic success, or great numbers of people converting to Christianity. Spirituality, in this instance, means a spiritual enablement within the person. Often this spiritual enablement is falsely related to spiritual maturity, but who wants another truth table?

In the table above, if this is one's orientation, results or success means the individual is spiritual. On the other hand, a lack of results (bottom right box) means a lack of spirituality (top right box). In this pattern the ONLY conclusion possible for evangelistic success is that the laborers are spiritual. No wonder people in "successful" Christian endeavors criticize the unsuccessful. The only way they can think is to brand the unsuccessful as unspiritual. The truth, however, is found in the completed table.

Spirituality	+	+	-	-
Success	+	-	+	-

Individuals can be spiritual and see results, spiritual and not see results, unspiritual and see results, or unspiritual and not see results. All of the options are possible.

You might wonder how unspiritual people can see results (especially if this broader and more accurate view of the truth is new to you). Actually it is simple and biblical. Success in endeavors is God's business (1 Corinthians 3:6-7). Also, Romans 1:16 says, "For I am not ashamed of the gospel of Christ, for it is the power

74

of God to salvation for everyone who believes, for the Jew first and also for the Greek."

The Word of God says that the power is in the gospel message itself. It is the power of God. Biblically this explains why evangelists or preachers with genuinely effective ministries are sometimes discovered to be morally bankrupt. They, and we, assume their success means the blessing of God on them, rather than what it is in truth: the message itself has God's power.

In Uganda, we saw in excess of 1,700 individuals come to faith in Christ (the most recent expedition from our church saw over 2,000). Were we more spiritual than those who remained stateside and prayed and funded the trip? I don't see how, or at least, I don't know. I trust we were Spirit-led and those at home were as well. The danger, however, is to equate our success with some "specialness" spiritually before God. This very thing is the mistake my missionary friends and many American Christians have made over the years.

Success Elsewhere Tempts Us To Unfairly Criticize Home, When The Real Point Is Mutual Encouragement

Why don't we see the same thing in America as we see in Uganda? We "missionaries" can also conclude that success in a distant land means something is wrong with our homeland. "Back home" environment, the people, or the circumstances are to blame as being unreceptive and spiritually blind. Quite frankly it could be any of these, but perhaps it's something else.

When you've been to another place and seen the gracious and mighty work of God, the last conclusion you'll tend to make is that it's you, that you're not spiritual or tuned in when back home. This, of course, could be the exact problem. A few years ago a man from a particular denomination wanted our church to start witnessing door-to-door "across the tracks" (in a poorer part of town). I asked him if he had shared the gospel first with those who knew him, for example, at work. He raised his voice and his eyebrows and said, "No way. Those people know what I'm like!"

That not withstanding, don't miss the point. I suspect we don't see the same results in America that we see in Uganda for many reasons. First, and foremost, we are not doing the same thing here as we do there (pray every day, offer the gospel as often as we can, organize ourselves to effectively give our lives to the lost, etc.). It may also be that Americans are inoculated; having a "little" of the disease of Christianity, and therefore avoid catching a real case of it.

Whatever the reason, I think being faithful at home is among the most wonderful and trying opportunities we face—and one for which the Lord will no doubt reward us in proportion to our faithfulness. Using results to determine spirituality is mistaken, and probably foolish. Criticizing others based on the falsely assumed connection between results and spirituality simply takes us away from the point.

We are invited **to encourage one another** to walk faithfully in God's grace, to grow into the likeness of Christ Himself, and to cheer for one another at every opportunity. A walk with God is for wherever we are; at home, at work, at play, and abroad.

I do believe in the enabling power of God to produce results through the empowered believer. With Watchman Nee, I suspect, and have observed, the "breaking of the outer-man" is directly related to the "release of the spirit", also known as a yielded or abandoned life—all of which is a great means through which God may reach out and reap a harvest.

The real point is not to busily critique and measure others, but rather to encourage one another in Christ. I am also in no way trying to critique others on this point. Instead I'm offering a nobler way to think about success in Christian endeavors through a lesson God highlighted in Uganda. Countless verses illustrate the point; none however, in my opinion, illustrate it as well as Hebrews 10:24-25:

> "...And let us consider one another in order to stir up love and good works. Not forsaking the assembling of ourselves together, as is the manner of some, but exhorting one another, and so much the more as you see the Day approaching."

I know this chapter is hard work, but what might happen if we take it to heart and cheer for laborers both at home and abroad? Something just might get done...and you, and others, will be the ones doing it.

Success Elsewhere Tempts Us To Unfairly Criticize Home, When The Real Point Is Mutual Encouragement

XI

THE WORD OF GOD CAN BE FRESH TO
AN OPEN HEART READY TO LISTEN

If you're a Christian, and if you are like me, sometimes your coke loses its fizz. You open the Bible and stare, or wander, or both, until you conclude you've tried enough and the effort itself counts for something.

Why is it that sometimes the Word is so fresh, while at other times it's so dull? I've concluded it is directly related to our willingness to listen. Listening is an act of the spirit and the heart of the human being. It is not about hearing in the simple mechanical sense of sound...to anvil...to stirrup...to cochlea...to nerve...to brain. When I say "hear", I mean it as Jesus meant it,

> *"He who has ears to hear, let him hear!"*
> *(Matthew 11:15)*

Hearing or listening in this sense is similar to taking a true breath. Recently my son and I were involved in voice body use lessons known as the Alexander Technique. In the training I was shown how to fully, naturally, and deeply breathe. The result was dizzying because I hadn't taken in that much oxygen in some time.

> *Do not love the world or the things in the world. If anyone loves the world, the love of the Father is not in him.*

Opening God's Word is much the same. I hope you've known moments when a truth comes at you so clearly and so profoundly that you're dizzy with the possibilities. I remember one such time in my early days with the Lord when I was listening through 1 John. When I came to chapter 2 and hit verse 15, it hit me back! He who loves the world...has not the love of the Father. In a moment of deep breath, of open ears and heart, I admitted I loved the world. I loved what money might do for me. I loved the senses and sensual pleasure. I loved what I might become in the world. Yet as I listened, I also concluded in a quiet moment from the shadows; I did not, I could not, love the Father. Sure I was a Christian and I loved God, but between the two, my love and interest in the world displaced my love and interest in the Father.

Displace is the right word...a careful word. I saw as I listened that either my love and affection could be on the Father, or it could be on the world. In either sense, whether the world is a wonder He made or a corruption that allures us away, loving it ends our love for the Father. As Romans 1:25 says, we can "worship and serve the creature rather than the Creator".

In my case, as I listened, I knew deeply and carefully what I wanted. I wanted the Father. I wanted to love Him above the world, above myself, above everything. In a dizzying instant my attention, my spirit, my heart, my love moved. I came to listen and I heard something I needed.

Please don't think I am saying this message is for you. This was a truth, a fact, an insight from God to me at a strategic place in my life. It was a moment in which I needed a word and a clarification from the Lord; and He delivered. Moreover, He delivered me.

What about you? I've noticed that most people who are serious about God's Word make a serious mistake. They rush and hurry and study hard, however, they miss the most important thing. They fail to take a truth deep into their own heart, because they happily skip over the surface, like a well-tossed pebble on the smooth green pond.

Are you one of those? Are you one among us who has studied much, who has become enthralled with each and every unusual fact you uncover, but remains unable to say the Word has really reached your heart? Imagine, if you will, what possibilities are available to the person who takes one pristine truth and drives it deep into her own soul over a week, or a month, or even a year. At the end of 12 years, this faithful soul would own 12 truths in a profound way; which, incidentally, must put her light-years ahead of the typical Bible student.

Listen. Drive deep. Fresh. These are phrases that come to mind as I try to share with you the full meaning of this chapter's title:

The Word Of God Can Be Fresh To An Open Heart Ready To Listen

Yes, it can be fresh. In my experience the freshness never leaves, but is revived every time I turn my focus on a precious passage God has put deep in my heart.

Romans 8:28-29 states,

> And we know that all things work together for good to those who love God, to those who are the called according to His purpose. For whom He foreknew, He also predestined to be conformed to the image of His Son, that He might be the firstborn among many brethren.

I can only see this passage with fresh eyes because of the way in which God has used it in my life. From the very first time I saw this passage through a pamphlet by Bill Bright, I have followed his recommendation which I will now share with you. In an event. In a difficult moment. Romans 8:28-29 states God's promise to work things together for good. The conditions or terms are simple.

It is for those who love God, and it is for the purpose of making the individual more like Christ Himself. Whenever I open this passage I can recount the magnificent ways God has blessed me through it. I recount the day our doctor told us our first pregnancy was over. I remember Jody experiencing labor pains, alone, and I out-and-about seeking pain medicine to ease her because the cost of an emergency room D-and-C was prohibitive. And then, just then, I thanked God for how He would work it to the good of making us more like His Son; and He did, I think, and gave us five more children. All healthy, all busy about the beach as I write these words. I see now, as a lover of God, how He has used His Word.

Just now I remember again the day I returned to our apartment and found the bedroom's sliding door ajar and footprints, muddy footprints, everywhere. Our sweaters, our bedspread, our new computer, our stereo, our music, our lives were carried away by thieves. In that moment, the verse was fresh again and I knelt by the bed, before making any call, and thanked the Lord for how He would work this to good. He did, in countless ways. All the stuff we had has been replaced a hundred times over and we added to our experience a deeper appreciation for the Father's care and our growing patience with what He allows and what He brings. Christ was patient and obedient that way. He learned it (Hebrews 5:8) and so are we learning it. Romans 8:28-29 is a fresh verse, as are many other verses He showed me as I read, or showed me through the faithful words of another.

In Uganda I watched this freshness appear. One morning as I thumbed through the book of Mark I came upon these words,

> *"But when they arrest you and deliver you up, do not*
>
> *worry beforehand, or premeditate what you will speak. But whatever is given you in that hour, speak that; for it is not you who speak, but the Holy Spirit."*

(Mark 13:11)

Of course, as a literalist, I know the verse was, perhaps is, for a special circumstance of persecution. However, I couldn't help but appreciate what role faith has played in my own life as a preacher. For too many years I followed the proper form of exposition using the tools of subject, complement, exegetical outline, homiletical outline, conclusion, introduction, seasoned-in illustrations, practice, present. I almost quit the ministry every week for years – until I found Phillips Brooks and Charles Spurgeon, who proclaimed the value of speaking in a fresh and Spirit-dependent way after much study and reflection.

The New King James Version says "don't premeditate". I've found this to be a powerful exhortation, not so much applied to the topic or passage, but to not premeditate the way I'll say it. This adds life and it adds me to the message itself (just as Luke is different than Peter is different than Paul). In that morning as I sat reading God's Word for freshness...I saw again what it means to trust God for the words...and I again let go of trying to refine and over-do my notes. Thanking the Lord, I prayed and gave Him the day.

It was later the same day. We have all returned from sharing the gospel hut-to-hut, and in that quiet part of the day before the evening crusade and after a very late lunch, we sit and sleep or read or relax. She was sitting, but she was not relaxed; a young mother who had left husband and children to follow God's call for a two-week adventure in Uganda. She looked hurt, brown eyes downward with tears welling up, and over, to race down both sides of her face. "Lisa," I said. She looked at me while trying not to. "What's wrong?" I pressed on. "I'm supposed to give my testimony and I'm scared to death," she said. I hadn't given much thought to what it means to these short-term missionaries to stand before a crowd of strangers and tell how God has touched their lives through His grace. Not only do they wonder if God has done enough to share, but they also fear losing the very ability to speak, or make sense, or both. "Lisa, this morning God allowed me to see a very important piece of comfort He offers those who speak for Him. I know the situation doesn't exactly match the passage, but see if He has something for you," I said as I steered her to Mark 13:11.

I stepped away and left her to the Lord and His Word, but I watched. I watched her read slowly and carefully and hopefully. Then, in a moment I saw freshness flood her, and a smile larger than a first quarter moon break joyfully across her face. She had found the Word to be fresh as it met her at a point of need.

Lisa spoke well that night and many were touched and came to know Christ that very evening. She had found in the Word a fresh insight for her own life which will be with her forever. And so it goes for any who approach the Word for fresh insight or refreshing appreciation for an old insight needed again.

God's Word indeed can be fresh. You simply need to bring your need and a heart ready to learn. In faith as you open His Word, He is able to make it fresh.

At the risk of having you not read the next chapter, I want to invite you right now to stop and pick up a Bible. Pray for the Lord to give you a fresh insight on your point of need (name it!) and open to any Psalm from 1-150. Read and watch what happens!

The Word Of God Can Be Fresh To An Open Heart Ready To Listen

XII

EMBARRASSMENT OVER WHAT YOU'VE BEEN GIVEN IS A GREAT STEP TOWARD FAITHFULNESS

The clothing styles in Uganda, at least in the villages, have been described by the following: Imagine a Salvation Army truck blowing up over Uganda.

It is a fair description as we saw a colorific amalgam of clothes worn by these people, except on Sunday, when they magically appeared with very nice outfits. We also contributed to the situation because we bring one-half of our luggage with the goal of leaving it. Yes, even though our efforts are fundamentally spiritual, we have a set of practical hopes as well. Old clothes, donated. Spare medicines and creams. Paper, pens, anything we leave is deeply appreciated.

All of our junk is a treasure in Uganda.

Consider how things might look through the eyes of a Ugandan child.

The Americans have come to share the Word of God and to bring us a church. Momma and Papa were so happy to see the workers building the church. Papa knows Musheke and Jonathan Samaali who came every day to make sure the workers did their job. Momma has not been happy, not at all, since the baby was taken away by the fever. I had the fever too, but Momma said I was too strong and God had things for me to do here. I'm glad for the church and I'm glad for Shanna and Amy, they are my friends and live in Texas, America. Today is so special because they each gave me their water bottles. Two. I have two bottles! I have more than any of my friends; and as I hold them, I think what a nice present it will be for my little brother, Kaifa. His eyes are bright and his smile very wide as we fill it with rocks. It is a rattle. It is Kaifa's rattle, and I sternly warn the others to leave Kaifa's rattle alone. What a joy to see these Americans who have come from so far to give us God's Word, and I am thankful for my bottle and Kaifa's rattle.

My point, of course, is overdone and overstated; but the fact is still there. We have so much. First, just physically we have so much. Homes and furniture and gadgets and electricity and phones and cars. By Ugandan standards we are all wealthy, but I say this as a fact to note, not as a club for our conscience. Spiritually we are blessed as well. We have literature, Bibles, buildings, and instant accessibility to spiritual input for our lives. A Ugandan might walk half a day to attend church, and a personal copy of the Bible is something special indeed!

Among the most consistent effects in the lives of those who go to Uganda, is a deep sense of overwhelm with how much we have and how blessed we are.

Here is the principle or lesson:

Embarrassment Over What You've Been Given Is A Great Step Toward Faithfulness

The word "embarrassment" is the right word and describes the exact feeling I had when I contrasted my life with theirs. Any solid cynic should just now point out how much better their lives probably are due to simplicity; working their own land, having time for reflection, etc. This, of course, is the sort of silly dreaming intellectuals do when they haven't lived enough to have perspective. At any rate, both the Ugandans and the Americans would agree—the standard of living in America is better from both viewpoints.

Embarrassment pulls up short of shame. I am not ashamed of being an American or a Southerner. I am not ashamed that God providentially placed me where He placed me. I am not ashamed that my ancestors participated in gross evils against my black brothers and sisters in the South (and in the Lord); anymore than I am ashamed that Noah (my ancestor) sinned. Ezekiel 18 makes it clear that each person will stand before the Lord and give an account for his or her own life. No parents or circumstance or ancestry can be blamed. Blame and shame belong to an undignified and will-less humanity. Neither you nor I belong to such a race or world. As an aside, the most humiliating and unbiblical action in our day is for various groups to seek compensatory tribute to "make up" for the crimes of the past. This sort of blame and shame game creates a slavery worse than the examples of history. It creates a helpless, will-less, irresponsible cadre of individuals who offer nothing to this needy world except a heritage of begging.

Shame, therefore, is not the right word. In Uganda, our friends, and brothers, and sisters, are not seeking compensation from Idi Amin. Instead, they are seeking an opportunity to provide for their families, live with some measure of health, grant their children an education, and walk humbly before their God.

Embarrassment, not shame is the right response; and it is a response that serves as a bridge to something greater. The embarrassment I mean here is the kind you can experience when you share with someone how many children you have, only to find they have unsuccessfully been trying to have children all their married life. This embarrassment mixes sadness with thankfulness. It is a soft and appreciative feeling that knows the flavor of undeserved and unearned blessing—especially in contrast to what else might have been.

It is a bridge, however, to greater faithfulness. Grace, in fact, often has this affect on those who truly receive it. Consider these passages:

> For who makes you differ from another? And
> what do you have that you did not receive? Now if you

*did indeed receive it, why do you boast as if you had
not received it?*

        *You are already full! You are already rich!
You have reigned as kings without us—and indeed I
could wish you did reign, that we also might reign with
you! (1 Corinthians 4:7-8)*

*For the grace of God that brings salvation has
appeared to all men, teaching us that, denying
ungodliness and worldly lusts, we should live soberly,
righteously, and godly in the present age.
(Titus 2:11-12)*

In the first example Paul is reminding the
Corinthians of God's gifts to them. God has graced
them to be different, and blessed, which leads in the
context to the simple fact that boasting and pride
disintegrate in the full light of acknowledging grace and
gift.

In the second passage we see the instructive
nature of grace on our very character. Many in our day
teach law and rules to (supposedly) keep the sin-bent
nature of humans in check. Paul, however, tells us that
grace itself is a transformational instructor.

When we see how much we have been GIVEN,
whether in physical blessings, spiritual gifting, or gaping
opportunity, we are thankfully embarrassed with a sense
of wonder as to why God gave to us and did not to
others. This insight is the bridge. It is the bridge you
can walk across to become faithful.

Take a moment to carefully read the parable of the faithful steward.

> Then Peter said to Him, "Lord, do You speak this parable only to us, or to all people?"
>
> And the Lord said, "Who then is that faithful and wise steward, whom his master will make ruler over his household, to give them their portion of food in due season? "Blessed is that servant whom his master will find so doing when he comes. "Truly, I say to you that he will make him ruler over all that he has. "But if that servant says in his heart, `My master is delaying his coming,' and begins to beat the male and female servants, and to eat and drink and be drunk, the master of that servant will come on a day when he is not looking for him, and at an hour when he is not aware, and will cut him in two and appoint him his portion with the unbelievers. And that servant who knew his master's will, and did not prepare himself or do according to his will, shall be beaten with many stripes. But he who did not know, yet committed things deserving of stripes, shall be beaten with few. For everyone to whom much is given, from him much will be required; and to whom much has been committed, of him they will ask the more."
> (Luke 12:41-48)

There is much to misunderstand here and much misunderstanding abounds. There are as many views as there are commentaries, but notice a few simple points.

1) Peter's question initiates this parable, and though Peter seems to hope the truths here do not apply to himself and the other disciples, an ounce of honesty declares this parable is for the disciples, and all other true believers.
2) The theme of the parable is reward for faithfulness, not works for salvation.
3) The point is best summed up for us in verse 48, *"For everyone to whom much is given, from him much will be required; and to whom much has been committed, of him they will ask much more."*

You have been given gifts, resources, and opportunities; not to bask in, but rather to serve with. Seeing what you have, using it to compare with others who have more, then feeling cheated; is a silly act of pride. On the other hand, seeing what you've been given in comparison to others can lead to that right kind of sobering embarrassment that can become the spark needed to become faithful.

My son Tripp, much to most people's surprise, has cerebral palsy. His palsy affects him in many subtle ways. He is limited in athletics, in musical instruments, and in many ways you probably take for granted in your child...he cannot perform. Tripp, however, is a genuine class act, and rather than seeing his limits, he sees how blessed he is by comparison. Tripp can think, and speak, and walk, and carry himself to Uganda to see God work through him. Many children with cerebral palsy are victorious if they can reach the lifetime accomplishment of putting peanut butter on a cracker.

What have you been given that you can be embarrassed about? What have you been given that, through your blessed embarrassment, can become your great step toward faithfulness? To whom much is given...make no mistake, that does mean you.

Embarrassment Over What You've Been Given Is A Great Step Toward Faithfulness

XIII

YOUR BROADEST CONTRIBUTION COMES WHEN YOU LIMIT YOURSELF TO YOUR GIFT AND TALENTS ALONE

"Two roads diverged in a yellow wood, and I, I took the one less traveled by, and that has made all the difference." So ends Robert Frost's most famous poem. The sentiment itself is profound and the very flavor of the words calls to something deep within most of us. "Yes," we say in some mystical reserve deep, deep, within. "Yes, I want to go a less traveled path and see with my own eyes, taste with my own lips, feel with my own heart, all that a different path offers me." Have you not seen this in your own life? Have you not noticed how much you long to be something other than average?

Many of our most spiritual and prolific Christian writers have spent much of their effort attempting to persuade us that such ambition flows from the self, the part of us that resists all that is of God and promotes all that is of us.

Allow me to offer a different possibility illustrated by the following passage:

> Then the mother of Zebedee's sons came to Him with her sons, kneeling down and asking something from Him.
>
> And He said to her, "What do you wish?"
>
> She said to Him, "Grant that these two sons of mine may sit, one on Your right hand and the other on the left, in Your kingdom."
>
> But Jesus answered and said, "You do not know what you ask. Are you able to drink the cup that I am about to drink, and be baptized with the baptism that I am baptized with?"
>
> They said to Him, "We are able."
>
> So He said to them, "You will indeed drink My cup, and be baptized with the baptism that I am baptized with; but to sit on My right hand and on My left is not Mine to give, but it is for those for whom it is prepared by My Father."
>
> And when the ten heard it, they were greatly displeased with the two brothers. (Matthew 20:20-24)

Here we see Jesus with a clear opportunity to rebuke the self in these disciples; but lo, He does no such thing! Consider the circumstance. Jesus has been teaching His disciples about His coming rule on earth [even after His resurrection He spoke for 40 days about this future rule (see Acts 1:3)]. In this part of the story the mother of these two men requests from Christ a great future for her own sons. Who can blame a mother for wanting a glorious future for her children? If you read carefully you'll find there is no evidence that Jesus thought the request was evil or selfish.

How about the sons? Were they selfish for desiring or not resisting the possibility of co-reigning with Christ? Were they weak men because their mother made a request for them? The answer is, "No"...or at best, "Who knows?" It is astonishing that so many Bible teachers have made such a big deal out of a simple fact the Lord understood intimately. Humans were designed by God to accomplish, to conquer, to multiply, to subdue the earth. No doubt this design has been corrupted, however, it doesn't negate the origin. The origin is the very image of God. Someday, if the Lord permits, I hope to pen a work on creativity, the central theme of which will be that when God made man in His Image, most of what we know of His Image is that He creates (see Genesis 1-3). If we are made in His Image then we are made to create as well. A great deal of energy is spent these days attempting to prove mankind doesn't "create", but rather that he merely "rearranges". It is quite a stretch to draw such a distinction, and upon inquiry, we find that the motive is to keep us from thinking we are [like] God. If we create, so the logic goes, we'll supplant our call with the gross error of making ourselves out to be God. This conclusion is however, only one possibility. In the classic nature of correcting errors, we can throw the proverbial baby out with the bath water. In this instance, the baby is thrown out instead of the water!

To create simply means to cause to exist. Something doesn't exist, then it does exist; that is creating. God created "out of nothing", which we might concede man cannot do. However, God then made man out of the dust of the earth which is tantamount to "rearranging". Man didn't exist, then he did. Perhaps if we pick a neutral word like "make" we can end this confusion. God **made** man, man **made** the pyramids. When humans make things, they are displaying the very image and God-likeness He ordained! Is this a good thing? Yes and No. When we create we are operating according to our design, however, this carries with it a kind of neutrality. Neutrality means we can create [make] for good or create for evil. Not unlike the will with which we can choose good or evil; our God-wrought interest in making, accomplishing, subduing, etc., can be motivated by a clean heart or a corrupted one. Our humanness or personality is Neutral...But. "Neutral" in that it is not right or wrong to possess the designs, preferences, and motivations that make us human. "But", we are bent to indulge appetites, lusts, and other forms of evil that have their roots in a good and God-honoring purpose. The most obvious example is sex, which God created as a desire within us. In the context of a committed monogamous marriage relationship, it is a wonderful and beautiful part of being human. In the corruption of rampant and serial sexual expression, it can be a germ-bed of final despair for the bankrupt individuals who violate, to their own demise, the sacred design of God.

How does this relate to the two sons in Matthew? Simply put, desiring to be at the right and left of the Lord was not rebuked as an evil action or want. Indeed, desiring eternal rewards is never presented as an evil in the Scriptures, on the contrary, it is presented as a proper aim for the faithful Christian (1Corinthians 9:24-27). Christ does not rebuke these men or their mother for the desire to reign with Him. Instead He simply checks their motives [are you willing?] and explains that it is not His to give. Case closed, issue over.

So why do we need this understanding that our desires, etc., are "Neutral, But"? We need this understanding to appreciate the point of this lesson:

Your Broadest Contribution Comes When You Limit Yourself To Your Gift And Talents Alone

We have a desire to excel, to accomplish, to contribute. Although this is an assumption and you might quickly show some counter example, generally this is an accepted fact (even the worst sluggard desires a meal or a drink). In order to excel at anything we must actually do that thing better than others. Imagine being in a footrace with others who run at your same speed. Everyone ties! It is just the same with any talent; no one excels at what she is merely average. It is this simple fact that we ignore. Most of us spend a terrific amount of energy, both mental and physical, attempting to improve our weaknesses.

Let's imagine for a moment that you work hard at your weaknesses. You labor and sweat and plan and chart. Each of your weaknesses gradually improves, and improves significantly. Finally, you measure these weaknesses, and to your amazement, they are no longer weaknesses. You've made it! You've moved each of these areas across the midpoint. These weaknesses are now average. You have slaved in order to become a broadly and notably average individual! Frankly, that's the best you can hope for.

Imagine another scenario. Rather than expending so much time and effort on your weaknesses, you focus on your strengths. A strength, of course, is something you are naturally good at...it comes easy to you. Strengths come in many shapes: athletics, spelling, hand-crafting, humor, etc. It can be almost anything and has the additional attributes of being enjoyable and energizing. Children tend to exhaust me, for example, but my wife has an endless energy for coordinating children into cooperative activities. She runs our church's AWANA (Bible memorization) Cubbies program. When she's there, it's smooth as glass; when she's gone...she's missed! Imagine putting effort into improving something you're naturally good at. Since you are already above average, that effort moves you to excellence. Indeed, you can excel at your strengths and become average with your shortcomings. If you want to excel, your strengths are the road to take.

The same holds for your gift. First Corinthians 12:7, 12 states it plainly concerning your gift from the Spirit,

But the manifestation of the Spirit is given to each one for the profit of all...

For as the body is one and has many members, but all the members of that one body, being many, are one body, so also is Christ.

The curious thing about your gift, however, is that specifically you are invited to serve with it <u>and</u> <u>not</u> with someone else's gift. This gift orientation keeps us interdependent in the Body of Christ. Some years ago I met a girl who was very new in the Lord and very excited about spiritual gifts. I asked her about her gift and she almost interrupted me, "Oh, I have this gift, and this gift, and this gift..." Then with eyes wide she exclaimed, "And I want them all!" I paused and then asked her, "Why would you need the church then?" She stopped mid-sentence, and to her credit said, "Hey, that's true. I wouldn't need anybody if I had all the gifts—so that can't be right!" Good for her, and good for you if you catch on here.

My conviction is that God has given each Christian only one gift. Some people have many talents, however, each believer has only one gift. Though I'm probably in the minority, I think Peter was making this point when he said,

As each one has received a gift, minister it to one another, as good stewards of the manifold grace of God. (1 Peter 4:10)

Perhaps you see it differently, yet if you'll recall the lesson from Chapter 8 about limits, you'll see the wisdom in assuming one gift. It gives you focus and intensity. For a few years in our spiritual gifts training we had trouble getting people to use their gift. The reason, it turned out, was because our approach left room for a grotesque combination of gifts. For example, what exactly is a faith-helps-mercy-discernment gift? Moreover, how does one develop it or how do others count on it? Even my dear friend Dr. Earl Radmacher (who believes in the possibility of multiple gifts per individual), observed that he had developed his gift(s) one-at-a-time. What wisdom.

I believe the Word of God and common sense both insist that your broad impact will occur through the gift and talents you can excel at—these very things come easy and energize you. They also are very noticeable by others...just ask your honest supporters for their take on your gift/talents.

Next, and this takes some daring, take one entire year and commit to limiting your focus to your best gift or best talent. Decide to make your life about serving with it alone. Refuse all else...and if need be, tell everyone exactly what you are up to. As a church, we've found much greater cooperation among ourselves when we openly admit and serve to our strengths.

The greatest example occurred for me in Uganda. From the moment we left to the moment we returned, I was fully supported in my gift. Though I am a pastor, my gift is preaching. In Uganda, I was kept from leadership and decisions and planning. My role was to preach the Word, which I did publicly at the crusades and in churches, and privately with the pastors and students in Uganda. My focus was to share the Word while others administrated and managed the effort. Moreover, the joy wasn't just with me. Encouragers were empowered to encourage, helpers to help, the merciful to show mercy—and amazingly it all got done. We touched Uganda together through our individual gift and talents.

Limits yield intensity and intensity will bring you excellence with your gift and talents. Ignore your weakness as much as you can, stretch to your strengths as often as you can; then, watch how God uses you to impact as broadly as you can...And thank Him!

Your Broadest Contribution Comes When You Limit Yourself To Your Gift And Talents Alone

XIV

YOU'RE REALLY ASLEEP WHEN YOU FAIL TO DREAM

The truth or lesson I'm offering here, at the end of this book, is a lesson I've observed in recent years which was highlighted in neon after I returned. In fact, the presence of this book in your hands follows more from this lesson than any other.

The ability to dream, the ability to envision, is a gift from God, and as Prometheus discovered by giving fire to mankind, a gift from the gods is a dangerous thing. We have known, or more accurately, a smaller sect of free men and women through the ages have known this lesson and used it to produce the greatest works in history; both the good and the evil ones. Some of these insights I've now come to appreciate after over-reacting to the perils of new age theories about thinking and envisioning. For many years I would only occasionally employ what I now know to be our birthright due to the Image of God; by which we exist, and live, through God's orders, to reflect His nature as His special creation.

We were made to create. We were made to make things. One of my dearest mentors, as well a friend, is Robert Fritz. His books <u>The Path of Least Resistance, Creating,</u> and <u>The Path of Least Resistance for Managers</u> come with my highest recommendation. He, as a composer and original thinker, spells out the profound dynamics of the creative process in a reachable way. These books are not specifically Christian, but they are specifically true. In my thinking, truth and Christianity are never enemies, but rather can often be the best of friends. Sad to say, however, they are far too infrequently introduced to one another.

In order to explain this lesson I want to offer a few images. The first image is from the carnival my family and I visit on vacation. It is a cheap-and-year-round carnival with a few rides for young children. She works there and I have seen her or her exact counterpart every year. Her shirt is dirty and she is too. She has kids, usually from more than one man, and they are in trouble. She lives every day just this way, though some nights she goes out and drinks until she wakes up somewhere else—her house, his house, no one's house; and she can't remember and her head aches like it often does from the hatchet of bad choices she keeps around for no particular reason. She goes home and puts on a t-shirt, smokes the first several cigarettes of today's pack or two, and goes off to work. She puts the children in the rides, tells them to keep their arms inside, and pulls a lever or punches a button, and it takes the children, my children around in circles and lights. They have fun and occasionally and briefly I see her smile and say sweet things to the kids for a moment of joy; but soon she is on break, in the back, smoking a cigarette or two so she can return to punch buttons and pull levers again.

The second image is from my morning on Saturday in Uganda. I sit in a thatch-roofed bungalow and they bring me my coffee as I look toward Mt. Elgon and write and study for the crusade that night and the sermon at tomorrow's dedication service. He is an old man, perhaps 40, but in Uganda age is decided by those who survive, and they are few because death knocks on every hut and house in that nation. He is mowing the grass, a green sea at least the size of a football field, but rounded and kissing the stately white wall that surrounds the grounds of the Mt. Elgon Hotel. He mows and I watch, struck by his method and his steady unchanging pace. He mows with a machete, a long blade I imagined as a kid was the maker of trails to civilization for the valiant-but-stranded explorer in the Dark Continent of Africa. I look at my first African man, wielding my first-seen machete, and he is mowing the estate's grass. He swings it low and level with a wide swooshing stroke, and the six-inch grass returns to an obedient two-inch height. He pauses after progressing to sharpen the blade, and repeats the steady swinging back-and-forth to mow a few more feet. Mowing this way will not take hours, but maybe days, and I am struck by the picture of the man with the machete as the picture goes through my heart.

The following are my unedited notes from this scene:

July 20, 2001; 10:30a.m.

    I am struck today, as I watch a man trim the grass with a machete; I am struck that I have been given a great and practical gift to use in this world. It is not a gift for the next life, as far as I know, but it is a great one for this life.

    The gift is the creative process, that is, the ability to create. The man with the machete represents so much of what I see here in Uganda. The methods are old, but they are adequate. He was using the machete to mow the grass as we would mow our backyard.

    The Creative Process can lead to a better way to mow. To curve a blade, to extend it, to build a motor. These improvements do not occur because there is no necessity. He is hired and he mows as he knows to mow.

    We could teach the Ugandan's of business and creating to fund the church from within Uganda!!!

    My burden is to look at myself and my life. In what way am I still "mowing with a machete" rather than envisioning something new and creating it? How could that <u>new</u> serve and <u>glorify</u> God? How could it open time for ministry or the spread of the gospel, or...?

    To clarify:

    I see many things in the village and a great variety of homes, possessions, wealth, etc. I also notice that the standards vary for Ugandans. They know what "nice" or "very nice" is because I see it in different homes and I see it in the Mt. Elgon Hotel. The hotel is "very nice" by Ugandan standards, but it is an old and dilapidated facility. Yet, as I live in Uganda, I feel it is _very_ nice!

In the human heart is a knowing of perfection. It is how we idealize and seek to improve and improve again. I think it is _the_ _very_ _thing_ God placed in our hearts to seek Him, who is the _true_ perfection!

I have come to believe that humans, by and large, choose to do or not do, because they have become convinced that they have no other choice. This may serve to good or bad. When a man chooses a certain course he believes it is the better course. This sounds like there is choice, but there is not!

If he believes that the choice is better AND he believes that taking a lesser option/choice is a foolish or evil thing to do—

Then he has only one choice! His only choice is to take the better option.

Of course, he is only aware of the options before him, and from these options, he chooses the better/best one!

What if we could think of options which are not options before us? What if we could think beyond what we currently see to choose from? Seeing other options gives us new possibilities for our choices and decisions. Indeed, giving people the gospel gives them the opportunity for a new choice: to believe in Christ!

God has given us an imagination that truly can add new choices. Many set their imagination on evil and devise many ways to sin, but it need not be this way for me.

What choices could I envision, what outcomes could I see, which are beyond my current situation or circumstance?

This is a gift. I can do this. God has given me both the ability <u>and</u> the understanding.

What, to God's glory, can I envision beyond <u>NOW</u> to bring into being...or to begin moving toward? What might I imagine that has been here-to-for unimagined? (Here I list personal questions about what things I might imagine.)

Some of this may not make sense to you because they are my notes and my endeavors in leading a church and preaching and writing and consulting businesses and creating inventions that are all pieces of my own life.

The lesson here, however, is about choice and freedom, and above all, about dreams. The ability to dream, to envision, to imagine, is the way out of any current situation. Dreams can be God-honoring or God-denying. The gift of dreaming, however, is still God's gift to mankind because we are made in His image.

Dreams can only come in three basic ways.

First, God can give a person a dream. The Bible is filled with these examples. One of the most outstanding dreams is the dream God gave to Moses for the freedom of Israel.

Second, dreams can come through our own ability to just "make something up", which is also from God, but in the form of an ability or capacity He endowed us with. King David used this ability when he dreamed of a magnificent temple for a dwelling place for God Almighty, the true King of both Israel and the Universe.

The third and final source of dreams is one passed from one person to another. In the case of David's dream of a temple, God permitted Solomon to embrace and fulfill his father's dream due to David's disqualification as a man with "bloody hands".

Why is dreaming so important? Dreaming is important because of choice. As mentioned in my private notes above, I've come to accept the fact that people almost always do what they do because they believe they have no other choices. Dreaming, envisioning, imagining brings new choices and new options to people. One of the most dramatic turnarounds morally in our nation is the increasing number of teens who are abstaining from sex until marriage. The single most important factor is that abstinence has been included as a viable option. A new dream was added to a world of voices that proclaimed, "kids will be kids", and "everyone's doing it". A new dream offered a new choice.

The lady at the carnival has no other choice, much like kids caught in the inner city, or others trapped in a world of addiction. No dream, no option, continued choice—the only choice available.

In recent years a Ugandan named Morris Ogenga, with his wife Aidah, and a handful of courageous elders in the Eastern Synod of the Uganda Presbyterian Church, began to dream. Whether it was from God or "just made up" due to the needs seen in the people, or the burdens enflamed by a careful study of the Scriptures, they brought their dream to the Lord. Just because we dream and have new choices, nothing guarantees God's approval. They brought this dream, a dream of planting new churches in the churchless villages of their region around Mbale Town, to the Lord.

> And whatever you do, do it heartily, as to the Lord and not to men. (Colossians 3:23)

> A man's heart plans his way,
> But the Lord directs his steps. (Proverbs 16:9)

> Delight yourself also in the Lord,
> And He shall give you the desires of your heart.
> (Psalm 37:4)

> And He was withdrawn from them about a stone's throw, and He knelt down and prayed, saying, "Father, if it is Your will, take this cup away from Me; nevertheless not My will, but Yours, be done."
> (Luke 22:41-42)

God is seeing fit to honor the dream in Uganda. In 3 years, Midland Bible Church alone has shared with 25,000+ Ugandans in villages, schools, and prisons...seeing over 5,000 converts. In the villages alone 5,000 Ugandans have heard the message of God's grace, with at least 2,500 of those placing their faith in Christ. In these villages, the churches which were established are vibrant and continue to this day in offering God's Word and love to their communities.

In fact, the choices beginning to arise in Uganda are expanding as people are catching the dream of new churches and the vision of new life in Christ. America, too, is seeing new choices rise up on wings, as churches, like ours in Midland, Texas, are dreaming and acting to see fulfilling the Great Commission become a present reality and growing orientation. Most of us had never considered serving in a true missionary endeavor because we thought we had no choice. A new dream, a new vision, brought a new set of possibilities that are changing thousands of lives, increasingly, all over the world.

What could happen if the lady at the carnival or the man with the machete would dream? Isn't it obvious? New choices would become available, and though they would not have to make a new choice, experience says they probably would.

Out of my dreaming came the opportunity to "fire" our missionaries, to begin again with missions, and to happily find Uganda. The lesson is simple:

You're Really Asleep When You Fail To Dream

Here is how the lesson works. **First**, dream, imagine, envision; prayerfully, and like crazy! Give all of these to the Lord and those He gives back, take the **second** step: look at everything that is currently true related to the dream. Your goal in the second step is to notice, and feel, the difference between where you want to be and where you currently are. This creative tension between where you are and where you want to be is vital, and becomes a key element in creating.

The **third** step is to decide to pursue the dream. In order for our actions to last, an actual choice is vital. The **fourth** step is to take your next best action. This step is most useful when it's something easy, but still moves you toward your goal. The reason something "easy" tends to be the most useful is simply that it sets you in motion. Momentum is always a big factor. By the way, the fourth step hasn't happened until you act.

The **final** step is to keep repeating steps one through four until you actually have your dream, or discover you can't have it by the will of God. In either event, you'll be in a new place, with a new standing from which to dream again.

The story of Uganda, our church, and our lives is the story of two dreams. In Uganda, Morris Ogenga was imagining a network of village churches filled with growing and maturing Christians, transforming the countryside and his country. In America, we were dreaming of a relationship with a country, the missionaries there, and many of us INVOLVED, offering the free gift of God's grace that has so wonderfully touched us. These dreams gave us new choices which led to new actions. Finally, the dreams

met together, and with many others we are seeing what we could only at first imagine. "Only imagining" is the very thing this principle is about; and not to be trumped by any creature, mortal or celestial, God stated through Paul...

> Now to Him who is able to do exceedingly abundantly above all that we ask or think, according to the power that works in us, to Him be glory in the church by Christ Jesus to all generations, forever and ever. Amen (Ephesians 3:20-21)

Yes. We are invited to ask, which means to pray. Yes. We are invited to think, which means to imagine. And in both efforts, however high we can take the prayer or the dream concerning what we might hope for in this life; God is able to do more, dramatically more, according to His power in us. Consider well the limits you create by your crouching prayers and your squatting dreams.

There is more, much more, to learn; but this lesson gives you all the start you need. What would it feel like to quit sleeping, to awaken, to dream? What could you dream about your marriage, work, children, church, spiritual life, friendships, etc.? What new choices would that new dream offer you? Finally, what lies just ahead, for your dream, as a new choice and the next step?

In His faithfulness,

Fred R. Lybrand
Midland, TX

POSTSCRIPT

Because of my own dreaming and God's mercy, I joyfully found a way to work "part-time" at Midland Bible Church (I still preach a full schedule) and begin my "full time" efforts at writing. This book would not be in your hands had I not dreamed, sought the Lord, seen new choices, and taken a first step. It also would not have happened without the help of many others. That's the beauty of this process. The Lord tends to bring others alongside who'd like to be a part of the dream as well. Thank you for being part of the fulfillment of my little dream; and please consider becoming a part of an effort like that in Uganda. Indeed, come join us through your church or organization. Also, please encourage others to purchase and read this book...just that act alone can greatly add to fulfilling the Dream for Uganda and other lands with those who are daring to dream.

APPENDICES

APPENDIX 1

Short-Term Missionaries with
<u>Midland Bible Church 2000-2002</u>

Amy Barker
Cheryl Barker
Gordon Barker
Hannah Barker
Lindsay Barker
Damian Barrett
Tyler Beard
Brian Behrman
Shannon Behrman
James Bobo
Sarah Bobo
Bill Boulton
Andrew Chapman
John Chapman
Aaron Close
Gary Cole
Amye Crass
David Crass
Jason Custer
Jonathan Custer
Christy Daniel
Craig Daniel
Earl Erwin
Marcia Erwin
Shanna Erwin
Lani Gillett

Dean Jarrett
Bobby Hall
David Hart
Glenda Hart
Jim Hillman
Jennifer Loftis
Phil Logsdon
Fred Lybrand
Jody Lybrand
Tripp Lybrand
Deborah McCurdy
Carrie Minor
David Minor
Sandy Minor
Lisa Muniz
Mike Muniz
Jessica Neff
Rose Painter
Connie Perrin
Mike Perrin
Angie Snell
Jon Snell
Roger Traxel
Mark Wilkin
Amy Woupio

APPENDIX 2

Midland Bible Church
(Our First Fund-raising Letter)

April 19, 2001

Dear Members and Friends of MBC,

I want to tell you straight out, we need your help.

First, please read the whole letter (there's a gift for you at the end). Also, if possible, please read this letter aloud as a family.

Twenty-one of your fellow Midland Bible Church family members are hard at work preparing to travel to Uganda, but the greatest hardship will be in raising the support necessary for the trip. Even though some of us can afford it, quite frankly others of us cannot. The Lybrands, for example, need to raise $ 9,000+ dollars (about $ 3,000 per person for Tripp, Jody, and yours truly).

Oddly enough it is the asking that is more challenging than any amount needed. We Americans are pretty self-sufficient (and private). Begging (or anything that feels like it) is a painful rub against the grain of our own sense of dignity or propriety. Additionally, it seems like a lot of money for a two-week trip.

The fact is, however, that we are going to do what almost no short-term "missions" trips in the world will do this year: We will plant a local church that will continue to do Christ's work for years to come. Most missions' efforts do good things: win souls, build buildings, feed the hungry, distribute literature, etc. Yet, how many can point to a lasting ministry which began with their presence and continues faithfully despite their absence?

Many missions' efforts are cheaper...and even nearer to home...but I know of nothing worthy of comparison to what God has invited us to do in Uganda. Consider three facts about MBC and this opportunity:

Freedom

We know "It was for freedom that Christ set us free" (Galatians 5:1 NASB). Perhaps to a fault, MBC has made giving an issue of personal freedom. You probably know that various churches, political parties, private "ministries", etc., pursue their patrons with a vengeance. In fact, an entire industry of companies exists just to persuade you to give to the particular charitable organization that hired them. We don't operate that way for one particular reason: The Word of God. "God loves a cheerful giver"(2 Cor. 9:7)... and if Grace and Freedom mean anything, they can certainly mean the most in our delicate areas. We believe God will move in the hearts of those He intends to have be a part of this effort. Slick strategies don't really move hearts, but shockingly they do move pens to write checks. Please don't give unless God moves you, but also don't give short of what God intends (even if it is to pay for a whole family!). Finally, realize that if we do not make you aware of the opportunity, then we have removed, by our silence, your Freedom to give.

Impact

"He is no fool who gives what he cannot keep, to gain what he cannot lose."

Jim Elliot, a man martyred in South America by the very people he was trying to reach with the gospel, penned these words. If the Bible is true, then the impact of your gift (something you cannot keep) can travel out from Uganda to the Throne of God where it will be remembered to your credit forever (something you cannot lose).

Besides God's delight and the personal impact on you in Forever, there is the practical side of God's work that will very likely happen in our plain view:

1. An enduring sister Church on the other side of the world will be established.
2. Hundreds of people will come to know Christ personally...some will probably even go to Him in death this year.
3. These new Christians will have a trained and experienced pastor ready to shepherd them.
4. These same people will go throughout their community each week as part of their training...openly bringing others to know Christ personally.
5. Some of the very ones we introduce to Christ will enter Bible College to be prepared to become pastors of future Churches.
6. The growing number of Christians in Uganda will become the parents, businessmen, and leaders of the

next generation in Uganda as a biblical lifestyle will prove out to be a key factor in increasing longevity.

7. The Ugandan Church, from its central location in Africa, may become the strategic point from which Christianity spreads throughout an entire continent.

8. We, who travel and serve under your partnership, will return to add all God has added to us to Midland Bible Church.

9. Midland Bible Church will continue to impact the lives of others, as we remain faithful and are further matured by God.

Friendship

Friendship, like the weather, is often mentioned but little understood. At the core of friendship is both attraction and commitment. We like who we like...and with time we usually like them even more. We also, when friendships ripen, add a commitment to the friend that often expresses itself in sacrificial service.

It is sacrificial service to get...shots, passports, training, time off, arrangements for kids, unafraid, etc., in order to go to the Ugandan mission field. Part of the motivation for those of us going is our friendship with you. It is our hope that God will impart to us, through the experience, spiritual blessings that we may bring back and share with you.

Our hope, as well, is that you will show your friendship to us with the sacrificial service of prayer, preparation, and personally giving from your resources. In essence, this is what being a "family of friends" really means.

Conclusion

The conclusion of the matter is rather simple. Pray for us. Invest through us.

Most of us are going to contribute financially for ourselves...but the blessing of watching the Body of Christ step forward to send us will encourage us beyond what you can really know.

Please consider giving to this project by May 13th, **Mother's Day** (at least an initial amount), to help us in our planning.

Even though you can give to the project as a whole, we actually want you to consider designating your gift to a specific individual (or individuals) you know. In a sense, it helps make their efforts personal to you as well. Of course, any overage will be distributed to the overall project. <u>Simply make your check out to Midland Bible Church and label it "Uganda"</u>.

Here are your Midland Bible Church missionaries:

...Names Listed

Finally, thanks for reading such a long letter. Here's the gift...you have my genuine permission to sleep through any one sermon, if you can!

With Permission from the Uganda 2001 Team and the Elders...

Grace and Truth,

Fred Lybrand

APPENDIX 3

How We Got To Uganda
(A Summary)

Our missionaries were indeed wonderful people. And though they met with varying degrees of success, it was really no fault of their own that we finally decided to "fire" them. When I say "fire", I mean that we gave each of our missionaries an entire year of support before we stopped our financial support relationship with them. The reason we needed to do this became obvious. First, we wanted to be involved in missions in a way that energized and excited the church. Additionally, we discovered that we wanted to be involved with planting churches, since our conviction is that churches are God's most highly favored way to promote His purposes in this world. Some of our missionaries were planting churches while others were not. However, what we found is that no matter how hard we tried to come up with a new "philosophy of missions", we were unsuccessful. We were unsuccessful simply because we were trying to create a match between our old missionaries and our newer thinking. One of the strange thoughts that we were willing to consider was the possibility of simply focusing on one country. Ideally, we wanted a place we could visit on vacation, keep up with all of the missionaries in it, and really saturate the church into a country. It would only take a little over 200 other churches to do the exact same thing to have the world covered. Instead, we had been having individuals scattered throughout the world in various endeavors, not particularly related to the church, though sometimes related to individuals within the church. Beyond that, there was no relationship established with a sister church in any of the foreign countries in which we were involved with missions.

During the interim, that is after we had ended our relationship with our missionaries, we continued to collect funds from our general giving to someday be directed towards missions. As we explored options, we ran into a few dead ends; opportunities that seemed great, but turned out to be uninterested in our direct involvement in the missions work. It seemed no matter where we turned, we were met with the idea that we "couldn't do" missions and should, instead, leave it up to the professionals.

In the midst of this entire process, we became disappointed with an opportunity we had pursued in Africa, in this instance, unrelated to Uganda. I had remembered from one of my frequent conversations with my friend from my very first Greek class at Dallas Theological Seminary, Dr. Keith Bower, that his church was involved with something in Africa. I called Keith in order to find out what they were up to and discovered that the head of the Presbyterian Church of Eastern Uganda was flying to the States within a few weeks of this call. Keith accepted our offer to fly up with Pastor

Morris Ogenga and visit with our Elders and others in the church to consider this opportunity. We accepted.

What we found was quite a surprise on many fronts. First of all, Pastor Ogenga and the Presbyterian Church in Uganda is a particularly Bible-oriented and evangelistic organization. We further learned that the vision for Uganda is to plant 10 churches each year. Unique to what I have understood about missions, Pastor Ogenga and the Presbyterian Church in Eastern Uganda had a growing and successful strategy. The strategy was first initiated and developed with the aid of Dr. Lew Wilson, who was serving at the time in a volunteer capacity with Keith's church, Grace Community Bible Church. Later, Dr. Wilson moved to head up evangelism at the gargantuan Second Baptist Church of Houston, Texas.

Grace Community Bible Church had already planted one church and was intending on planting two more churches during the upcoming summer. We were invited to send an initial team to be a part of this strategy, to "fact find" in order to consider how the Lord might lead us to be a part of the effort in Uganda. I had been under the misapprehension that, even though there was certainly a move of God in the African continent evangelistically, all that was needed was a tree and a meeting time and a teacher of some type in order to have a "church". I have since learned that the Ugandans are indeed people just like us, and expecting them to consistently grow and develop as a community of believers without a physical and a permanent facility is just as ludicrous in Uganda as it would be for us here in

America. The strategy being used in Uganda is as follows. First, pastors are being trained in a Bible college context there in Mbale Town, which is the local hub from which the churches are being planted in the various villages. As the men are ready, the hope is to supply churches for them to begin to pastor. Wisely, the leaders in Uganda generally attempt to place a Bible college graduate in an already established church while moving a more seasoned pastor to the new church plant. Having an available pastor, however, is not all of the strategy. First, land is bought and an actual church building is built on the site within the village the leaders have prayerfully chosen for the church plant. A team from America arrives and is involved in a simple process throughout a week at the church site. First, each evening there is a crusade held with music, testimonies, and preaching from the Word of God. All of this is facilitated by Ugandans; however, the testimonies and preaching are performed by us Americans through a Ugandan translator. Even though Uganda was under British rule and has English as its national language, there are many dialects and many levels of education; therefore, a translator helps to make the message all the more clear. The crusade, however, is not the only means of reaching the village. During each day, we Americans are sent out to walk through the village from hut to hut or house to house to share the good news of Jesus Christ. But first we go in groups of twos or threes; however, by the end of the week, everyone is more than willing to go at it alone, though always we are with a translator for the hut-to-hut evangelism. By the end of the week, the entire village has been able to hear the message of the gospel. Hundreds and hundreds of people have come to faith in Christ and on Sunday morning, a packed service is held commissioning the new pastor by the laying on of hands and prayer and by a charge from Pastor Ogenga to the people and to the pastor to be faithful to the great work God has begun. When we leave the situation, we have left where there was nothing but a building, a collection of believers in Christ Jesus ready to be grounded in the Word of God and ready to be faithful to share the good news with their friends and neighbors in this new community that has a permanent church with a godly pastor and the opportunity to fellowship and worship and study in their own village.

APPENDIX 4

Our Process for Uganda

✓ We send the funds in advance to purchase property and build a church building, house, and fund the new pastor for a year.

- This generates interest and ownership as the building goes up in the village in time to be officially opened upon our arrival and labor. It also provides stability as a permanent structure with a part-of-the-community shepherd right there.

✓ We select the participants, not simply whomever wants to go, but (prayerfully) those who have shown faithfulness already in their lives.

✓ We prepare with general training about travel, Uganda, and our schedule of activities.

✓ We prepare specifically by becoming proficient in sharing the gospel of grace, especially using EvanTell's "You Can Tell It" training by Larry Moyer.

✓ We raise the money through making the opportunity and needs known, both within the church and among our friends and family abroad. We've always seen the money amazingly show up to meet the opportunity.

✓ We go to Uganda for about a two week stay.

- We are daily in the village sharing from hut-to-hut.
- We are nightly on the church grounds with the crusade (music, testimonials, teaching/preaching) for the gathered village.
- Some of us take turns visiting the schools and prisons on various days.

✓ We return home and tell everyone what happened, hoping to steal a few quiet moments to reflect deeply on what we experienced and learned.

✓ We evaluate the trip, make adjustments, recommit to next year, and begin new preparations.

APPENDIX 5

Resources

For Additional Copies of **About Life and Uganda**
www.trafford.com/robots/02-1299.html
Or call toll free 1-866-232-4444

To receive a packet of information about the different needs and opportunities in UGANDA, or about how you or your church can participate, please send your inquiry to:

uganda@midlandbible.org
Or
Midland Bible Church
2800 North A Street
Midland, Texas 79705
1-915-684-9722
Or
Grace Community Bible Church
5121 F.M. 359
Richmond, Texas 77469-9120
1-281-341-0618

Interest in training for effectively explaining the Gospel may be found at:

EvanTell, Inc.
P.O. Box 741417
Dallas, TX 75374-1417
1-800-947-7359

To inquire about Mr. Lybrand speaking to your organization or church please contact:

> *Tina Jacobson*
> *The B&B Media Group*
> *1-(800)-927-0517*
> *tjacobson@tbbmedia.com*

Printed in the United States
By Bookmasters